Making Mathematics Accessible to English Learners

A Guidebook for Teachers

Grades 6-12

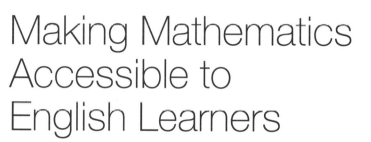

John Carr, Cathy Carroll, Sarah Cremer, Mardi Gale,
Rachel Lagunoff, and Ursula Sexton

Printed in the United States of America.

ISBN: 978-0-914409-68-7
Library of Congress Control Number: 2009925737

The book cover is printed on 50% recycled paper. The text paper is certified by the Forest Stewardship Council and the Sustainable Forest Initiative.

WestEd, a national nonpartisan, nonprofit research, development, and service agency, works with education and other communities to promote excellence, achieve equity, and improve learning for children, youth, and adults. WestEd has 16 offices nationwide, from Washington and Boston to Arizona and California. Its corporate headquarters are in San Francisco.

WestEd books and products are available through bookstores and online booksellers. WestEd also publishes its books in a variety of electronic formats. To contact WestEd directly, call our Publications Center at 888-293-7833.

For more information about WestEd:

Visit www.WestEd.org

Call 415-565-3000 or toll free 877-4-WestEd

Write WestEd at 730 Harrison Street, San Francisco, CA 94107-1242

Contents

Figures

Tools and Strategies

Preface

We developed this guidebook for middle and high school mathematics teachers who are looking for a practical, easy-to-use approach to help English learners in their classrooms understand the rigorous mathematics content reflected in state standards. Mathematics teachers at the elementary school level should also find the strategies in this guidebook relevant and useful, although the content of specific examples will not always reflect elementary school standards. This guidebook for mathematics teachers is based on its predecessor, *Making Mathematics Accessible to English Learners: A Guidebook for Teachers*, published in 2007 by WestEd. We have created common instructional strategies between the mathematics and science guidebooks to encourage and support cross-discipline collaboration between mathematics and science teachers, and consistent learning experiences for their students.

The guidebook is intended as a resource for teachers, to be used with district instructional materials within a district program that includes ongoing professional development, collegial discussions, and coaching. It is our hope that teachers will have opportunities to practice the guidebook's strategies in their classrooms, discuss them, observe one another practicing them, and become increasingly adept in choosing and combining strategies within their lesson plans. Because this kind of learning develops over time, we urge schools and districts to plan the ongoing time and support necessary for teachers to successfully adopt and implement a comprehensive approach to differentiating instruction for English learners and other diverse learners.

Thank you to the persistent content area teachers who prodded us over several years to create resources for teaching content area subjects to English learners. We can only hope this is the kind of resource they had in mind.

ACKNOWLEDGMENTS

We were very fortunate to have the advice of a number of experts in mathematics instruction and the instruction of English learners in the development of this guidebook. Their generosity in formally reviewing the manuscript and offering numerous comments and suggestions resulted in many refinements that became part of the final product. We hope that the guidebook reflects their collective wisdom.

REVIEWERS

Veronica Aguila
Administrator, Instructional Resources Office,
California Department of Education

Sylvia Celedón-Pattichis
Associate Professor of Language, Literacy,
and Sociocultural Studies, University of
New Mexico

Marta Civil
Professor of Mathematics, University of
Arizona

Debra Coggins
Mathematics Coach, Bay Area (CA)
Coalition for Equitable Schools

Jivan Dhaliwal
Mathematics Coordinator, Santa Clara
County (CA) Office of Education

Mark Driscoll
Co-Director, Education Leadership Center,
EDC, Inc.

Jim Greco
Education Program Consultant, Mathematics
Science & Leadership Office, California
Department of Education

Kathlan Latimer
Program Consultant, Mathematics Science
and Leadership Office, California Department
of Education

Miriam Leiva
Founding President, TODOS:
Mathematics for All
Distinguished Professor of Mathematics
Emerita, University of North Carolina,
Charlotte

Roslyn Lewis-Chambers
Mathematics Coach, Washington Preparatory
High School, Los Angeles (CA) Unified
School District

Silvia Llamas-Flores
PhD Candidate, Mathematics Education,
Arizona State University

Noemi Lopez
Marketing Manager, Communications and
Public Information, Harris County (TX)
Department of Education

Bob McDonald
English Learner Mathematics Teacher, Marc
T. Atkinson Middle School, Cartwright (AZ)
School District
Membership Chair, TODOS:
Mathematics for All

Steve Schneider
Director, Mathematics, Science, and
Technology Program, WestEd

Margaret Stark
PhD Candidate, Mathematics Education,
Arizona State University

We welcome your feedback, as well; please write to us at info@WestEd.org, or contact us through
www.WestEd.org.

Introduction

Every classroom includes students with diverse learning needs and interests, and this diversity is increasing as more English learners enter our education system.[1] Within the population of English learners, there is also considerable diversity. As Kathleen Flynn and Jane Hill assert, "No two [English learners] are the same."[2] English learners differ from one another in their native languages, levels of English language development, prior experiences, and formal education. Like other students, English learners may prefer particular learning modalities and styles, may be designated for special education services, or may have a special interest in mathematics. Since no single instructional method works for all students, effective teachers continually explore and experiment with new ways to engage all students in successful learning. They learn to differentiate instruction to meet students "where they are" and to help them all achieve the same set of standards.

Although it is challenging to teach a rigorous mathematics curriculum in ways that ensure English learners can understand the content and demonstrate what they have learned, it is certainly possible. This guidebook provides practical tools and strategies that allow middle school and high school mathematics teachers to help their English learners become literate in mathematics, think and express themselves like mathematicians, and perhaps develop the skills and passion to become mathematicians.

For all students, a large part of learning mathematics is learning the language of mathematics and using mathematics terminology meaningfully within academic conversations and written work. Understandably, students who are simultaneously learning the English language and mathematics need extra support. Hands-on and authentic, problem-based instruction works best for English learners, and mathematics pedagogy fits well with this approach.[3] This guidebook presents concrete tools and strategies that address the language aspects of mathematics instruction, and capitalize on the visual and experiential aspects of mathematics that benefit all learners, especially English learners.

For teachers who have participated in professional development related to working with English learners or who have read professional books and articles about best practices for teaching and assessing diverse learners, we expect that many of the ideas presented here are at least somewhat familiar. We have pulled together the best ideas, tools, and strategies from a variety of sources[4] and pointed out their interconnections. The practical format, which includes plenty of description and examples, prepares teachers to use these strategies in the classroom. While designed to benefit all teachers, the guidebook will be particularly helpful for teachers who are monolingual in English, have no bilingual classroom aides, and have English learner students at various levels of English listening, speaking, reading, and writing proficiency.

The guidebook offers teachers an integrated approach to teaching mathematics content and English language skills that enables English learners to access content and express their mathematical thinking. According to Arieh Sherris, such an approach "is task-based and focuses on the knowledge, skills, and academic language within a content area. The academic language includes the concepts, key vocabulary, grammar, and discourse necessary to accomplish content-area tasks."[5] Our approach to teaching English learners is similar to popular models such as Cognitive Academic Language Learning Approach (CALLA)[6] and Sheltered Instruction Observation Protocol (SIOP).[7]

While effective mathematics teachers are also language teachers, few mathematics teachers have had extensive training in the pedagogy of English language arts or in English language development (ELD). Ideally, the responsibility for effectively teaching English learners is shared among teachers in a school who recognize ways to coordinate English development across subject areas. We urge mathematics teachers to collaborate with English and ELD teachers to build the academic language of the English learners they share. The English and ELD teachers can offer teaching suggestions, insights about particular students, and instructional help with specific skills, such as note taking or writing a report on a long-term project, that English learners must master in conjunction with mathematics concepts.

Finally, we encourage all teachers in a school to work together to provide a uniform, consistent instructional approach with core instructional strategies. Truly effective instruction that results in proficient high school graduates is a long-term, schoolwide, team effort.

ENDNOTES FOR INTRODUCTION

[1] Flynn, K., & Hill, J. (2005, December). *English language learners: A growing population*. McREL Policy Brief. Accessed February 24, 2009, from http://www.mcrel.org/pdf/policybriefs/5052pi_pbenglishlanguagelearners.pdf. See National Clearinghouse for English Language Acquisition and Language Instruction Educational Programs (NCELA) for national and state demographics over time. Accessed February 24, 2009, from http://www.ncela.gwu.edu/stats/.

[2] Ibid., p. 4.

[3] Dominguez, H. (2005). Bilingual students' articulation and gesticulation of mathematical knowledge during problem solving. *Bilingual Research Journal, 29*(2), 269–295.

[4] Sources are cited when ideas, tools, and strategies are introduced in the chapters that follow. Three major citations are:
Marzano, R.J., Pickering, D.J., & Pollock, J.E. (2001). *Classroom instruction that works: Research-based strategies for increasing student achievement*. Alexandria, VA: Association for Supervision and Curriculum Development;
Hill, J.D., & Flynn, K.M. (2006). *Classroom instruction that works with English language learners*. Alexandria, VA: Association for Supervision and Curriculum Development; and
Richard-Amato, P.A., & Snow, M.A. (2005). *Academic success for English language learners: Strategies for K–12 mainstream teachers*. New York: Longman. (Authors of several chapters are cited in this guidebook.)

[5] Sherris, A. (2008, September). Integrated content and language instruction. In *CALdigest*. Washington, DC: Center for Applied Linguistics. Accessed November 12, 2008, from http://www.cal.org.
Another source is Ellis, R. (2003). *Task-based language learning and teaching*. Cary, NCa: Oxford Applied Linguistics.

[6] Chamot, A.U., & O'Malley, J.M. (1994). *The CALLA handbook: Implementing the cognitive academic language learning approach*. Reading, MA: Addison-Wesley.

[7] Echevarria, J., Vogt, M., & Short, D.J. (2008). *Making content comprehensible for English learners: The SIOP® model* (3rd ed.). Boston: Allyn & Bacon.

CHAPTER 1
Teaching Mathematics

This chapter offers an overview of mathematics instruction that is effective for diverse learners, particularly English learners. We begin with three principles of learning and motivation that apply to all learners. Then we describe an inquiry-based approach to mathematics instruction that has fidelity with National Council of Teachers of Mathematics (NCTM) standards.[1] We end the chapter with a description of how to use various modes of instruction for English learners.

PRINCIPLES OF LEARNING AND MOTIVATION

Regardless of whether students are native English speakers or English learners, three research-based principles about how people learn[2] guide effective mathematics teaching and learning. These principles are the foundation of all of the ideas and strategies presented in this guidebook. Making mathematics accessible to English learners means, first of all, recognizing how any student learns.

Principle 1. Students come to the classroom with preconceptions about how the world works. If their initial understanding is not engaged, they may fail to grasp the new concepts and information that are taught, or they may learn them for purposes of a test but revert to their preconceptions outside the classroom.

English learners, like any learners, need a way to connect what they know with what they need to learn.

Principle 2. To develop competence in an area of inquiry, students must (a) have a deep foundation of factual knowledge, (b) understand facts and ideas in the context of a conceptual framework, and (c) organize knowledge in ways that facilitate retrieval and application.

English learners, like any learners, need to learn facts and ideas and need to be able to relate and organize them conceptually.

Principle 3. A metacognitive approach to instruction can help students learn to take control of their own learning by defining learning goals and monitoring their progress in achieving them.

English learners, like any learners, benefit from reflecting on their learning goals and progress. English learners, unlike native English speakers, will need to apply a metacognitive approach to learning English, as well as to learning discipline-specific content — in this case, mathematics content.

The artful teacher brings these principles to life for each student, recognizing a student's current level of knowledge and understanding and facilitating each student's growth as a self-directed learner. A respectful classroom climate is key to a teacher's success in being able to do this.[3] Often a visitor can step into a classroom and feel a distinct climate, whether of respect and caring, fear of ridicule, or boredom and detachment. A positive climate is established by teacher modeling and facilitation and is sustained by student practice.

When teachers nurture a safe learning community within their classrooms, students respect each other's ideas, are patient with one another, recognize there can be multiple perspectives and ways of learning, and recognize the value of individual contributions to group learning. With their anxiety lowered, students are physiologically more able to accept new challenges and grapple with new concepts and problems.[4] Because English learners can be expected to feel high levels of anxiety about all the challenges they face, it is especially important for them to feel respected by the teacher and other students, whether they are struggling to learn English and mathematics or to communicate different cultural perspectives they may bring to discussions.

Within inclusive classrooms, educators increasingly recognize that equitable and equal are not synonymous. Widespread interest in differentiating instruction reflects the understanding that students learn in different ways. Providing a high-quality mathematics education for all students means planning and using strategies that fit diverse students. Inquiry-based mathematics education meets these goals for providing equitable access to the curriculum for all students, including English language learners.[5]

AN INQUIRY-BASED APPROACH TO MATHEMATICS EDUCATION

When taught well, mathematics requires students to solve problems, reason, and communicate. Effective mathematics teaching "engage[s] all students in:

> » Formulating and solving a wide variety of problems

> » Making conjectures and constructing arguments

> » Validating solutions

> » Evaluating the reasonableness of mathematical claims"[6]

The instructional strategies described in this guidebook offer teachers a way to involve English learners in an inquiry-based, language-rich approach to solving mathematical problems. An inquiry-based approach to mathematics instruction for English learners explicitly targets content and language objectives, and is implemented through various instructional methods, including student inquiry and teacher modeling.[7] Inquiry-based instruction is rooted in constructivist learning theory and capitalizes on students' curiosity by offering hands-on, *authentic* activities and tasks (Principle 1 of learning and motivation). An authentic problem is one whose context is interesting or meaningful to students, whether they are working on a word problem connected to real-world experiences or a purely mathematical problem.[8]

Teachers begin lesson planning for inquiry-based mathematics instruction by identifying key mathematics standards and related mathematical ideas (Principle 2 of learning and motivation). Students systematically acquire knowledge as lessons progress through these connected or overlapping mathematical ideas. During classroom instruction, the teacher models mathematical thinking and guides students' understanding of the interrelationships among mathematical ideas. Throughout the learning process, the teacher monitors student thinking and involves students in reflecting on their own thinking (Principle 3 of learning and motivation).

To introduce a mathematical idea, the teacher poses an engaging, intellectually challenging task or problem. Students are then guided to use mathematical reasoning to reach conclusions about the task; to justify their conclusions; and to generalize about them.[9] The teacher also instructs students in such cognitive tasks as judging effects of mathematical operations, understanding mathematical properties, and making connections among mathematical concepts. As part of this cognitive guidance, the teacher models mathematical language and appropriate ways to discuss mathematical problems.[10] As one teacher remarked, "All of my students — English learners and native speakers — need to learn the language of mathematics and use that language to discuss their mathematics reasoning about real problems."[11] The development of these skills builds the foundation for and supports effective social learning.

Social learning[12] is an integral part of inquiry-based learning and can be effective for English learners[13] when the teacher models target language and discussion expectations, provides visual language supports (e.g., Word Walls, Sentence Starters), and monitors and guides students as they work collaboratively in small groups. Social learning is effective because it promotes a rich environment for the use of academic language, such as problem-solving discussions that require use of mathematical terminology. Students are expected to practice purposeful listening and speaking skills. As they work in small groups, English learners hear their peers rephrase what the teacher has said and discuss their ideas, with the support of visuals and hands-on activities.[14] During small-group activities, the teacher monitors students' academic, social, and English language learning as they propose and try alternative problem-solving strategies, and explain their conceptual thinking through speaking and writing. In a supportive classroom, English learners benefit from a variety of such collaborations, which offer repeated opportunities to participate in discourse that builds their mathematical and literacy knowledge.[15]

In spite of what we know about effective instructional practices, mathematics continues to be taught in some classrooms as it has been traditionally: As a fixed body of knowledge and set of procedures. Students are asked to reproduce mathematical expressions, but are rarely expected to produce innovative solutions to mathematical problems. As a result, students achieve automaticity in reproducing mathematical expressions or performing computations, but do not develop *mathematical literacy*. Individuals are considered mathematically literate when they can use mathematics as a fully functioning member of a society.[16] This includes the ability to read and understand mathematics content in newspaper articles (e.g., pie charts, line graphs, data tables, averages, percentages, and sampling error in polls) and use mathematics in everyday tasks.

When instruction focuses on having students simply manipulate mathematical expressions and practice algorithms, it avoids the important cognitive challenges of understanding word problems and discussing mathematical ideas. This type of approach is generally not effective for any learner, but it is especially problematic for English learners because it does not involve them in the mathematical thinking and talking that support both language development and mathematics learning.[17] Specifically, they do not learn to identify the important facts in a real-world problem, select an appropriate strategy to solve the problem, and explain their reasoning. The ultimate consequence is that English learners become marginalized in mathematics education and do not have the opportunity to become mathematically literate or choose a math-oriented career.

To elaborate on the recommendations for English learners in mathematics classrooms, we present a list of best instructional practices for English learners in mainstream mathematics classrooms:[18]

> » Provide a rich, meaning-centered context for students to use language, with many visual representations, hands-on activities, and language supports.

> » Provide ample opportunities for high-quality interaction between English learners and native English speakers that encourage English learners to share their knowledge and experiences, hear other students rephrase what the teacher said, and apply new language.

> » Use high-frequency vocabulary that students know and gradually introduce more academic vocabulary as they progress in the lesson and their language skills.

> » Integrate listening, speaking, reading, and writing skills across instruction, and assist English learners to make a bridge between oral and written language.

In order to help students advance as learners of mathematics and of the English language, these strategies blend direct teaching and student inquiry,[19] and are implemented in the context of high-quality mathematics instruction.

THE 3-PHASE MODEL OF TEACHING AND LEARNING MATHEMATICS

Although the mathematics community has not reached consensus about what to call them, it is common practice among research-based mathematics curricula to organize lessons into three phases.[20] During the first phase, often called "introduce" or "launch," the teacher encourages students to draw on their prior knowledge in order to engage with a new concept. In phase two, "investigate" or "explore," students work with the new concept in the form of a meaningful problem. During the third phase of a mathematics lesson, "summarize" or "wrap-up," students and teachers draw conclusions and make connections to related concepts.

In this guidebook, we use *introduce*, *investigate*, and *summarize* to label the three phases, as reflected in Figure 1.1. Note that student assessment is continuous throughout the three phases because teachers use feedback from assessment to adjust instruction during all phases. Each of the three phases is described below,[21] followed by an excerpt[22] of a teacher's vision for implementing that phase in the classroom.

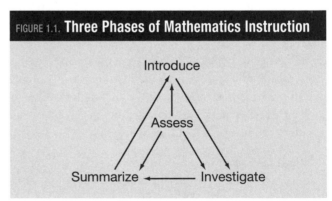

FIGURE 1.1. **Three Phases of Mathematics Instruction**

Introduce

The learning process begins as the teacher guides students to make connections between the learning task at hand and their past academic, personal, and cultural experiences. The goal is to engage students in learning by sparking their curiosity, posing intriguing problems, or asking thought-provoking questions. This phase also offers the teacher opportunities to identify students' preconceptions and misconceptions about a mathematical concept. When misconceptions arise, they are simply acknowledged along with other brainstorming ideas, but the teacher mentally notes these misunderstandings to ensure that they are explicitly addressed at the proper time.

As part of this phase, it can also be useful for a teacher to make explicit the mathematics and language objectives that are the focus of the lesson. For example, as part of the SIOP® model,[23] the teacher presents these objectives to students orally and in writing. Doing so makes it crystal clear to students how the planned discussions and activities will address mathematics standards and English language standards.[24] (Language objectives specific to a lesson may be derived from charts of Academic Language Skills that are presented in chapter 3.) When the teacher makes learning objectives explicit, it helps all students focus on the "bull's eye" from the start of the lesson; and it sets the basis for students to reflect on how well they achieved those objectives at the end of the lesson. The teacher plans a lesson that targets those specific content and language objectives, and reflects after the lesson on how well the instructional strategies and learning activities stayed on course and met the objectives.

> **In my classroom . . .** I begin my lesson plan with an intriguing idea, image, or question to engage students. I pose questions about what my students already know, make conjectures about how to solve a problem, and encourage students to pose questions about what they want to learn. This alerts me to what students already know, their misconceptions, and areas of potential confusion. I let students know at the start of each lesson what our mathematics and English language objectives are so that students understand the purpose of the activity.

Investigate

The teacher guides students as they investigate a mathematical task, work toward a common understanding of specific concepts, and acquire problem-solving and computational skills. The teacher designs activities that encourage students to construct new knowledge or skills, propose preliminary ways of thinking about a problem, "puzzle" through problems, and try alternatives to reach a solution. As students engage with the mathematics, the teacher encourages them to demonstrate or explain their conceptual understanding of the problem and the process skills they used to arrive at their conclusion. Students debate alternative explanations for their conclusions and use new facts to correct their prior misconceptions. As appropriate, the teacher directs students' attention back to helpful points from the introduce phase of instruction. Students are guided to organize information supporting their ideas or conclusions into evidence-based statements, using mathematical language.

> **In my classroom . . .** Rather than telling students the concepts I want them to learn, I expect them to think critically about the concepts by experimenting, investigating, observing, classifying, communicating, measuring, predicting, and interpreting. This active engagement arouses their curiosity and leads them to discover new ideas, confirm prior assumptions, or reconsider their earlier thinking.
>
> I guide students to explain their thinking by asking questions and facilitating peer discussions. I give students time to think, and I facilitate student–student discussions to correct misconceptions. I provide time to question and justify answers. I do not just answer questions that students pose, nor do I simply decide for them which answers are right or wrong. By

listening to their ideas and reasoning, I can determine the next instructional experiences I want to provide students.

Summarize

The summarizing phase involves more than just revisiting what has been learned. During this phase, the teacher engages students in activities and discussions that challenge and extend their conceptual understanding and problem-solving skills. Students apply what they have learned to new mathematical tasks and experiences to develop, extend, connect, and deepen their understanding of the concepts.

> **In my classroom . . .** At the end of an instructional unit, I help students compare, contrast, combine, synthesize, generalize, and make inferences by asking them to solve a problem or perform a task that introduces a somewhat different context from those they have just experienced. I want students to be able to apply new knowledge, make connections, and extend ideas. Their various ideas for applying their knowledge help me to differentiate instruction better so that all students can engage in activities.

Assess

Throughout the three phases of inquiry-based mathematics instruction, the teacher assesses students' progress and asks students to evaluate themselves. Feedback may come from quick, on-the-spot checks for understanding (e.g., expressed with hand gestures, white boards), quizzes, student discussions, journals, or other techniques. The teacher uses the feedback to reflect on how effective a lesson was, and to make mid-lesson adjustments to better meet students' needs and interests. Students use the feedback to reflect on what they understand, what they still need to learn, and what they want to learn next. (See chapter 6 for a fuller discussion of assessment strategies and uses.)

> **In my classroom . . .** I test students on more than just factual knowledge; during an assessment, I challenge students to construct ideas and explanations, just as I do during classroom instruction. I want assessments to reflect both my objectives and the content standards.

Throughout each phase of mathematics instruction for English learners, the role of the teacher is multifaceted and ever changing. As a facilitator, the teacher nurtures creative thinking, problem solving, interaction, communication, and discovery. As a model, the teacher initiates thinking processes, inspires positive attitudes toward learning, motivates, and demonstrates skill-building techniques and the effective use of language to communicate mathematical thinking. Finally, as a guide, the teacher helps to bridge language gaps and foster individuality, collaboration, and personal growth. The teacher moves flexibly into and out of these various roles, as appropriate for each lesson.

Figure 1.2 identifies aspects of what the teacher and the student may be doing in each of the three instructional phases. Assessment methods (which appear in italics) encourage students to assess their understanding and abilities, and they provide opportunities for teachers to evaluate student progress. All teacher and student activities listed below are especially important for English learners.

FIGURE 1.2. Three-Phase Model for Teaching and Learning Mathematics

Purpose	How the Teacher Is Engaged	How Students Are Engaged
Introduce		
To initiate the lesson: » Connect students' past and present learning experiences » Anticipate new ideas » Focus students' thinking toward the mathematical goals of the lesson. Mathematics and language objectives are stated orally and posted on the wall.	» Create interest and generate curiosity » Raise questions and problems » Ensure students understand the mathematical purpose of the activity » Elicit responses that uncover students' current knowledge about the concept/topic » *Refer students to existing data and evidence and ask, "What do you already know?" "Why do you think…?"**	» Asking questions such as "What do I already know about this question?" "What are the parts of the question that I need to use to answer the question?" "What problem-solving strategies can I use to answer the question?" » Showing interest in the topic » *Discussing understanding with peers*
Investigate		
To provide students with experiences within which mathematical concepts, processes, and skills are identified and developed.	» Guide students to work together » Observe and listen to students as they interact » Provide time for students to puzzle through problems » Redirect students' investigations as needed » Guide students to explain concepts and definitions in their own words » Suggest definitions, explanations, and new vocabulary » Elicit mathematical justification from students » *Observe and listen to students as they apply new concepts and skills* » *Ask open-ended questions such as "What evidence do you have?" "How did you think about the question?"*	» Thinking creatively within the limits of the task » Forming, testing, and refining conjectures and strategies » Trying alternatives to solve a problem and discussing them with others » Explaining possible solutions or answers to other students » Generating definitions and explanations of concepts » Listening critically to and respectfully questioning explanations from the teacher and from other students » Connecting to previous activities » *Answering open-ended questions by using observations, evidence, and previously accepted explanations*

* Italics indicate assessment methods.

FIGURE 1.2. **Three-Phase Model for Teaching and Learning Mathematics (continued)**		
Purpose	**How the Teacher Is Engaged**	**How Students Are Engaged**
Summarize		
To make mathematical connections and extend students' conceptual understanding and skills.	» Help students understand alternative explanations and make connections among mathematical ideas » Encourage students to apply the concepts and skills in new situations » *Assess students' conceptual understanding and knowledge/ skills* » *Look for evidence that students have changed their thinking* » *Look for evidence that students are deepening their understanding*	» Applying new labels, definitions, explanations, and skills in new but connected situations » Drawing on experience to ask questions, propose solutions, make decisions, and present reasonable conclusions based on evidence » *Demonstrating an understanding or knowledge of the concept or skill* » *Evaluating own progress and knowledge* » *Asking related questions that would encourage future investigations*

* Italics indicate assessment methods.

This three-phase approach to mathematics lessons is related to a similar approach in science education. Our broad intent is for mathematics and science teachers to see commonalities in the mathematics and science guidebooks, and to collaborate on instructional practices. The three instructional phases in mathematics education correspond to the five stages of inquiry-based science instruction described in Roger Bybee's "5 Es" model (see Figure 1.3). A description of the teacher's role during each of the five stages follows.

1. Engage: Activates students' prior knowledge and preconceptions, relates concepts to students' interests

2. Explore: Guides students to investigate a phenomenon

3. Explain: Supports students to identify and discuss explanations for scientific phenomena

4. Elaborate: Guides students to apply learned concepts to new experiences to extend and deepen understanding

5. Evaluate: Evaluates students' progress and adjusts instruction to fit student needs.[25]

Both instructional models can provide a deeper understanding of the teacher's role in an inquiry-based classroom. The 5 Es of science instruction are more fully elaborated in the research than are the three phases for mathematics lessons; Appendix A includes a full description of this model for inquiry-based science teaching and learning.

FIGURE 1.3. Mathematics Phases and Science Stages

3 PHASES IN MATHEMATICS	5 Es IN SCIENCE	
Introduce	Engage	Evaluate
Investigate	Explore	
	Explain	
Summarize	Elaborate	

Source: Carr, J., Sexton, U., & Lagunoff, R. (2007). *Making Science Accessible to English Learners: A Guidebook for Teachers*. San Francisco, CA: WestEd.

THREE MODES OF INSTRUCTION APPLIED TO ENGLISH LEARNERS

Throughout the phases of mathematics instruction, teachers commonly combine three modes of instruction — teacher-directed, teacher-assisted, and peer-assisted (see Figure 1.4). In a mathematics classroom, each of these modes offers students distinct learning benefits and opportunities. Adjustments to each mode can further enhance English learner engagement and understanding.

Teacher-directed. English learners will feel comfortable during teacher-directed instruction when the teacher provides comprehensible input,[26] using language and speech students can understand, and supporting it with visuals and demonstrations.

Teacher-assisted. English learners will feel more comfortable speaking in teacher-assisted conversations when the teacher establishes a risk-free, caring climate and takes students' proficiency levels into account when expecting them to comprehend input and produce meaningful output.

Peer-assisted. English learners will feel comfortable in peer-assisted instruction when respected and supported by peers in the group and when group tasks are within their communication capabilities. Peer-assisted instruction is an opportunity for English learners both to use their native academic language (if grouped by same language) and to participate as English listeners and speakers as key concepts are repeated and rephrased in English during whole-class discussion.

Teacher-Directed Instruction

In teacher-directed instruction, the teacher provides direct instruction to the whole class, and individual students respond to the teacher; most interactions are teacher–student. The teacher initiates concept development by giving direct instruction, demonstrating to the whole class, and modeling specific mathematical protocols and expected behaviors and processes. The teacher combines saying with showing — supporting oral instruction with pictures, illustrations, manipulatives, relevant objects, graphic organizers, models, demonstrations, video clips, and other visuals. Teacher-directed instruction gives students access to the information they need to process and manipulate ideas, clarify concepts, and build the connections among concepts that lead to greater understanding of mathematics.

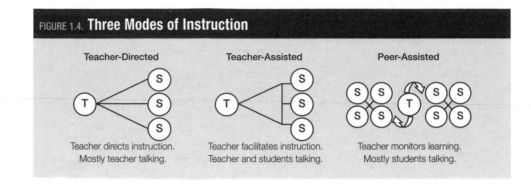

FIGURE 1.4. **Three Modes of Instruction**

Teacher-Directed	Teacher-Assisted	Peer-Assisted
Teacher directs instruction. Mostly teacher talking.	Teacher facilitates instruction. Teacher and students talking.	Teacher monitors learning. Mostly students talking.

APPLICATIONS FOR ENGLISH LEARNERS

Teacher modeling is an important support for English learners. English learners need to preview completed projects and writing assignments; some students may never have had formal schooling or participated in similar tasks in their former countries. Similarly, before students engage in teacher-assisted discussions and peer-assisted learning activities, the teacher needs to model expected discourse and social behaviors and procedures.

When speaking to students, the teacher can target the listening abilities of English learners in terms of enunciation, speed, intonation, and use of vocabulary, idioms, and contractions. For example, English learners at novice levels require simple subject-verb-object sentences, free of idioms and colloquial expressions. (It can be surprising how many expressions such as "no way," or "make up your mind," or even "take a seat" pepper typical classroom instruction, to the befuddlement of English learners.)

For the benefit of English learners as well as other students, all teacher-directed instruction should be divided into chunks no longer than 15 minutes. Students need time to process each chunk before encountering another chunk;[27] they must relate new information to their prior knowledge and experiences, address any prior misunderstandings, and construct new understandings. English learners may also need extra time to process spoken information, so they can listen in English, think in their primary language, and translate their thinking back into English. In some instances they may also want to discuss unfamiliar English vocabulary and new mathematics concepts with someone who speaks their primary language.

Between chunks of presented material and information, the teacher checks for students' understanding. Research indicates that learning improves for the whole class and the achievement gap narrows when the teacher uses techniques to get feedback about each student's understanding during direct instruction and immediately makes appropriate adjustments.[28]

Calling on individual students is a way for the teacher to collect feedback from a few students at a time. Alternative ways to check for understanding can provide a broader range of information and encourage all students to respond:

» Students use white boards to write and display short answers.

» Students signal agreement/disagreement/confusion with a point of view, solution, or approach, using colored cards or hand gestures.

» Students answer chorally.

» Students work in teams to respond. For example, teams contribute to a collective class solution to a problem; or partners talk with one another in English or their primary language before reporting to the class in English.

When asking a question of the whole class, the teacher waits several seconds so that all students have ample opportunity to process the question and think about an answer (three to seven seconds depending on the difficulty of the question). The teacher may acknowledge early hand raisers with a nod while still waiting to give everyone time to think of an answer. This wait time allows English learners to decipher the question, think, and formulate an answer in English. It also encourages more students to respond. To resist the urge to keep the lesson pace moving rapidly, the teacher may use a technique such as counting silently or pacing the floor one step per second. When the teacher calls on a student, walking close to the responding student may lessen the student's anxiety about speaking in front of many peers. When English learners hear other students rephrase information during responses, it provides additional opportunities to learn mathematics vocabulary and comprehend important ideas.

Teacher-Assisted Instruction

In teacher-assisted instruction, the teacher guides brainstorming and discussion among the whole class, through interactions that are student–student and teacher–student. For example, in the Think-Pair-Share activity, pairs of students quickly share an idea based on the teacher's question; then the teacher facilitates whole-group sharing and discussion of students' responses. (See chapter 5 for strategies to facilitate and scaffold student work and discussion.) Grouping students in different ways will help support students' language development and confidence in the classroom. (Figure 1.5 illustrates one teacher's grouping decisions.)

In this mode, the teacher does not lecture and give answers. When a student asks a question, other students respond rather than the teacher. Small groups or the whole class agree that an answer is correct, appropriate, or applicable based on supporting evidence and reasoning. Teacher-assisted instruction empowers and guides students to think and talk as mathematician apprentices. Through thoughtful questioning techniques, the teacher facilitates and probes to encourage critical thinking; responds to student questions with meaningful questions that engage them in further dialogue with each other and with the teacher; and promotes the revision or review of their interpretations based on the evidence at hand. As students construct meaning from their explorations and text, the teacher may deem it necessary to intervene — by providing further evidence, raw data, or other resources or interactions — so as to model closer examination of evidence to correct misconceptions. By providing a safe environment in which to express ideas, the teacher allows students to consider alternative interpretations and test new ideas, while continuing to build understanding based on empirical and quantitative evidence.

FIGURE 1.5. **One Teacher's Grouping Decisions**

Following is a brief scenario of a high school mathematics classroom where the teacher shifts among teacher-directed, teacher-assisted, and peer-assisted instruction. This scenario shows the advantages of grouping students by their primary language. Other grouping criteria should be used as well (e.g., social characteristics, topic choice, mathematics literacy).

Classroom setting. I speak only English and I have 35 students in my class, most of whom are English learners, representing five languages (Spanish, Vietnamese, Mandarin, Tagalog, and Russian).

Grouping. Often I plan flexible student groupings for mathematics tasks, mixing students by primary language, English literacy, and/or mathematics literacy. Other times I allow students to select their own groups, and they usually select friends who speak their language. Today, I allow students to self-select, and most do so by their primary language.

Modeling. I start by posing an authentic context to the class. I give directions to be sure students understand the expectations of the task and model some of the discourse I expect of students involved in this task. I point to sentence starters on the wall that scaffold English learners to articulate their thoughts (e.g., "I agree with ___ that..."; "What if we..."; and "I think that...").

Group learning. Then student groups talk about and complete their tasks. Discussions within the self-selected groups of English learners are typically a mix of English and primary language, depending on the group members' needs and comfort levels. For example, a group of English learners mixes Spanish and English during their discussion, with the more advanced English learners rephrasing certain ideas in Spanish for a very limited English learner who is showing difficulty understanding the English. I walk around to answer questions and ensure that they are all learning successfully. Later, when I model the English responses to the questions, all students — even the most recently immigrated English learners — must write in English. Later, when we have the full-class discussion in English, the most limited English proficient learners will have a good idea of what is being said because it was first discussed within the homogeneous language group.

The advantage to having students use their language of choice for peer-assisted learning and problem solving is that the focus stays on the mathematics content. Students are not inhibited by their varying abilities to communicate in English, so I feel more comfortable that they can really understand the concepts in the day's activity. However, many times I form heterogeneous groups by mixing more proficient and limited English learners with different primary languages so students must use only English to convey their ideas, and the more proficient English learners and native English speakers are models for the limited English learners.

Discussing. Next, I lead a whole-class discussion in English about what they did and said. I use the same structured format every time: (1) What strategy did you use to solve the problem? (2) Did you discover more than one strategy to solve it? and (3) How are the strategies that have been presented similar/different? I write students' answers as English sentences, projected so that they all can see. Students copy the sentences in their notebooks in English and make connections to their own solution notes. I find that repetition of common questions helps orient my English learners and provides a familiar context.

My newest student, who is at the *beginning* English learner level, benefits from listening to good oral models about content that is both familiar and meaningful, although I do not expect him to fully comprehend all that other students are saying. I assist other English learners to communicate their ideas by providing vocabulary, cues, and other structures that help them convey their thinking. The more proficient the English learner, the more elaborate I expect his or her comments to be. I do not ask "dumbed-down" questions, but I do adjust questions to be comprehensible for my English learners. When they finish responding, I selectively rephrase answers to model mathematics discourse and incorporate key vocabulary. This mathematical rephrasing benefits all students in the class.

Source: McCall-Perez, Z. (2005). *Grouping English learners for science*. Unpublished manuscript. Adapted with permission.

The teacher ensures that English learners can participate in a variety of ways. First, the teacher frequently combines manipulatives or visuals, such as word walls (see chapter 5), with teacher talk, emphasizing key words and concepts. English learners can easily glance at word walls to find words they want to use when they answer questions or participate in class discussions. Second, the teacher uses controlled speech, tailoring the wording of some questions for novice English learners, and adjusting some for intermediate and more advanced English learners. Differentiated questioning gives all students the opportunity to participate in rich class discussions.

When an English learner student responds (and the answer moves the discussion forward), the teacher may use "mathematical rephrasing" to clarify the idea for all students and model desired academic discourse. For example, if an English learner says, "*y equal x square* ($y = x2$) *is* a curve," the teacher might respond, "Yes, the graph of *y equals x squared* is a parabola (drawing or pointing to it), a line that curves." The rephrasing is most helpful to the English learner if it is just a level above what the student produced independently. The student may choose to repeat the teacher's rephrased statement, but should not be asked to do so. Mathematical rephrasing helps all students gradually develop much more sophisticated academic discourse skills. This can happen in a safe, respectful environment because students feel comfortable with their classmates and recognize the importance of everyone's contributions to group learning. When English learners are involved in class discussions where many students repeat the important terms and ideas, they have a greater opportunity to comprehend concepts and thought processes. To support this kind of learning, a teacher might invite students to indicate their agreement by restating the teacher's or another student's statement.

In teacher-assisted instruction, before asking individual students to reply, the teacher may use Think-Pair-Share, to give students ample time to think and share answers with a partner before the whole-class discussion begins. This allows English learners to express their ideas comfortably with a partner before "going public" in front of the class. Think-Pair-Share is another way to build in repetition because it allows English learners to hear an important concept described in slightly different ways, first in pairs and then in a whole-class discussion.

Peer-Assisted Instruction

In peer-assisted instruction, small groups of students interact and learn as a team through collaborative or cooperative activities. Before students begin complex group activities, the teacher may need to model the expected group learning behaviors and establish rules of conduct. Students teach each other and learn together while the teacher monitors, guides, and models as necessary.

Some basic steps prepare students to work effectively in teams or small groups and ensure that English learners will be able to participate and learn. To design effective cooperative and collaborative activities the teacher makes sure that an activity is cognitively challenging for everyone, while varying the language demands students must meet in order to participate and contribute. The activity is also structured to be what Elizabeth Cohen[29] would describe as "group worthy," meaning that it necessitates collaboration and discussion.

By setting clear directions and expectations for group work, the teacher sets the best conditions for students to focus on learning. In classrooms with English learners, directions should be written as well as oral. When the teacher writes the directions before giving them orally, it provides an opportunity to check that they are clear.

Sometimes students working in groups misbehave or become passive because they do not understand the concepts or the task instructions. To remedy this, the teacher may need to initiate group work by modeling expected behaviors and gradually shifting ownership of the group learning process to the students. Assigning roles is one way to help groups manage their interactions and structure successful participation for everyone. For example, a novice English learner in a group could participate as the illustrator of key concepts, while more English proficient students are assigned to act as facilitator, writer, or reporter. As they gain more experience and success, students can choose their own roles or collaborate more interdependently. Regardless of how groups are structured, teachers should set the expectation and provide the opportunity for all students to learn and accomplish the goal of the lesson.[30]

Grouping decisions should serve the teacher's strategic goals. Grouping English learners by primary language; including an English learner in a group with more proficient English speakers; grouping students by characteristics other than English proficiency; or allowing students to choose groups by topic or interest may help some students feel more comfortable speaking in the group. In a classroom where a strong community has been established, students might sometimes be allowed to choose groups by friendship, as long as everyone understands that no student should feel unwanted. Often, teachers assign novice English learners to a group with a proficient English speaker so that the English learner hears language modeled and other students' rephrasing of what the teacher said.

The size of a group matters. Pairs and triads are more likely to keep all members involved. Foursomes or larger groups may provide more opportunity for diversity of ideas or be necessary because of the number of available resources (e.g., manipulatives), but one or more students may become marginalized or choose to be passive. Cooperative tasks in which each student is assigned a specific subtask can keep all students involved in a larger group such as a foursome. A teacher might start the year by guiding students to collaborate in pairs and then make the transition to triads and foursomes.

DIFFERENTIATING INSTRUCTION

Differentiating instruction[31] means using a variety of instructional strategies that target the diversity of students in the classroom — students with different learning styles, interests, special needs, and those who are also English learners. For English learners, differentiation means tailoring a specific strategy to fit their various levels of English proficiency. It does not mean creating an individualized lesson for each student. It means planning a variety of ways for students to interact with new concepts. It also means controlling speech and using word walls, visuals, and small-group learning activities to make input more comprehensible for English learners.

For example, a mathematics teacher who has English learners at two or three levels of proficiency (see chapter 3 for a description of English language development levels) may use the same teaching strategies for all students, but differentiate instruction by offering support that is tailored to students' levels of English language proficiency with a given strategy. When required to record their thinking, all students are encouraged and supported to draw pictures or write sentences. When students are expected to write several connected sentences, the teacher gives English learners templates with some portion of the text already completed, according to their language level. The most novice English learners receive a template that only requires filling in key words and phrases or drawing diagrams to express their thinking. English learners at a higher proficiency level are provided sentence starters and transition words between sentences to help them write connected ideas. (See chapter 5 for a more detailed discussion of such supportive strategies.)

Other ways the teacher can differentiate instruction for English learners include: Accompanying oral presentations with visuals to help students listen with greater comprehension; giving English learners note-taking outlines or sentence starters to help them capture key concepts in a challenging textbook; and providing hands-on activities to help English learners "see" and actively engage in learning mathematics concepts and procedures. When the teacher presents the big picture or main idea first, as a frame for the information that will follow, English learners are better prepared to concentrate on what is most important. It is important that direct instruction for English learners be delivered in small chunks, allowing them time to process the information. Connecting instruction to students' experiences and offering varied forms of support heighten all students' interest and personalizes instruction in a way that motivates students.

Some students learn better in small groups than they do individually. Small group talk gives English learners a chance for language repetition and practice, so differentiation also means planning for collaborative and cooperative learning activities. The focus of differentiation is to be aware of all the ways students are different from one another, and to plan to teach in ways that capitalize on those differences. The classroom techniques described in Figure 1.6 reflect a number of the ideas in this chapter about differentiating instruction for English learners.

FIGURE 1.6. **Supporting English Communication for English Learners**

The following classroom techniques have been found effective in supporting English communication and differentiating instruction for English learners:

» Tap into prior knowledge to give students richer context for what they will learn. At the same time, activating prior knowledge lets students anticipate vocabulary and terms they are likely to hear and enables them to use context to guess words they do not know.

» Provide wait time after asking a question — it may take English learners extra time to process back and forth in their primary language and English as well as to understand the question itself.

» Have students discuss with a partner or in small groups relevant information from prior mathematics lessons or personal experience; monitor group discussions; and then use a few examples to share with the class. Use flexible grouping in terms of primary languages spoken, English proficiency, general mathematics knowledge, friendships, and other criteria.

» Use multimodal presentations — visuals, word walls, graphic organizers, hands-on activities, etc. — during direct instruction and when summarizing or reviewing.

» Repeat and rephrase important concepts, keeping periods of lecture or reading brief and concise but highly contextualized. Present new words in the context of the lesson and apply words during the lesson, pausing to emphasize each key word.

» Use tiered lessons that address the same standards and topics but that adjust the language level to challenge without frustrating students. For example, plan opportunities to restate a chunk of oral instruction in simpler form for English learners, perhaps while other students do seatwork; provide texts at different reading levels; assign tasks that differ in language demands; assign learning activities to small groups in which more proficient English speakers rephrase concepts and English learners are assigned less language-demanding, but still mathematically rich, parts of the task.

During assessment, the teacher also differentiates. For example, if students are to write about what they have learned, they are not uniformly presented with a blank sheet of paper and the general direction to "Explain the Pythagorean Theorem and its application in the real world." It will be more appropriate to ask some English learners to respond orally to a series of guiding questions. Others may be provided with sentence starters or graphic organizers, or be asked to draw pictures with labels and write a few simple sentences that explain their pictures. Often the scaffolding strategies that are used to help English learners during instruction also are used to help them express what they have learned during assessment. Figure 1.7 presents an example of assessment differentiation that scaffolds English learners at different levels of proficiency.

In chapters 4 through 6, the ideas explored in this chapter about the three-phase model, modes of instruction, and differentiation of instruction will be made more concrete, as we introduce specific tools and scaffolding techniques that support English learners. Chapters 2 and 3 present information about language acquisition and expected skills at each language proficiency level, to provide

FIGURE 1.7. Assessment That Accommodates Different Levels of English Proficiency

In the example below, the teacher provides assessment accommodations at three levels of English proficiency. The goal is to learn as much as possible about what English learner students have or have not understood about mathematics content, not to demonstrate that they are not yet proficient in English.

Beginning. English learners are given a template and asked to visually represent key ideas in pictures, diagrams, or graphic organizers. Students include complete simple sentence starters and labels as appropriate to their level of language development. (See chapters 2 and 3 for descriptions of various levels of language development.)

A quadrilateral has 4 sides. Some quadrilaterals are parallelograms or have parallel sides (II), but some are not parallelograms. A trapezoid is a type of_____. A trapezoid has at least one pair of _____ sides. The shape of a roof of a house looks like a _____.

Intermediate. English learners complete a visual representation and also complete sentence frames that help them connect ideas.

A quadrilateral has 4 sides. If the sides are parallel (II), the quadrilateral is a _____. If the sides (of the quadrilateral) are not parallel, then… A trapezoid is an example of…

Source: Carr, J., Sexton, U., & Lagunoff, R. (2007). *Making Science Accessible to English Learners: A Guidebook for Teachers*. San Francisco, CA: WestEd.

mathematics teachers with a firm foundation for embarking on strategies to effectively teach English learners at different developmental levels. In chapter 2, we provide a brief overview of language acquisition theory as it applies to classroom practice; and we compare the cognitive demands of learning conversational English with those of learning more formal, academic English. In chapter 3, we describe students' language abilities at five levels of English proficiency using a simple chart, and list an array of corresponding teacher strategies.

ENDNOTES FOR CHAPTER 1

[1] Martin, T. S. (Ed.). (2007). *Mathematics teaching today*. (2nd ed.). Reston, VA: National Council of Teachers of Mathematics.

[2] National Research Council. (1999). *How people learn: Bridging research and practice*. Washington, DC: National Academies Press. See also NRC's *How students learn: History, mathematics, and science in the classroom* (2005).

[3] Chapin, S., & O'Connor, C. (2007). Academically productive talk: Supporting students' learning in mathematics. In W. G. Martin, M. E. Strutchens, & P. C. Elliott (Eds.), *The learning of mathematics: Sixty-ninth yearbook* (pp. 113–128). Reston, VA: National Council of Teachers of Mathematics.

Boaler, J., & Humphreys, C. (2005). *Connecting mathematical ideas: Middle school video cases to support teaching and learning*. Portsmouth, NH: Heinemann.

[4] Weiss, R.P. (2000, July). Brain-based learning: The wave of the brain. *Training & Development*, 20–24. Accessed February 6, 2006, from http://www.dushkin.com/text-data/articles/32638/body.pdf.

[5] Hawkins, B. (2005). Mathematics education for second language students in the mainstream classroom. In P. Richard-Amato & M.A. Snow (Eds.), *Academic success for English language learners*. New York: Longman.

Padron, Y.N. (1993). Teaching and learning risks associated with limited cognitive mastery in science and mathematics for limited English proficient students. *Proceedings of the third national research symposium on LEP student issues: Focus on middle and high school issues.* (Vol. II.) Washington, DC: U.S. Department of Education, Office of Bilingual Education and Minority Languages Affairs.

[6] Martin, T. S. (Ed.). (2007). *Mathematics teaching today.* (2nd ed.). Reston, VA: National Council of Teachers of Mathematics.

[7] National Research Council. (1999). *How people learn: Bridging research and practice.* Washington, DC: National Academies Press.

National Council of Teachers of Mathematics. (2000). *Principles and standards for school mathematics.* Reston, VA: Author.

Hawkins, B. (2005). Mathematics education for second language students in the mainstream classroom. In Richard-Amato, P.A., & Snow, M.A. (Eds.), *Academic success for English language learners*, (p. 380). White Plains, NY: Pearson Education, Inc.

[8] National Council of Teachers of Mathematics. (2000). *Principles & standards for school mathematics.* Reston, VA: Author.

[9] Martin, T. S. (Ed.). (2007). *Mathematics teaching today.* (2nd ed.). Reston, VA: National Council of Teachers of Mathematics.

[10] Boaler, J., & Humphreys, C. (2005). *Connecting mathematical ideas: Middle school video cases to support teaching and learning.* Portsmouth, NH: Heinemann.

Khisty, L.L., & Chval, K.B. (2002). Pedagogic discourse and equity in mathematics: When teachers' talk matters. *Mathematics Education Research Journal, 14*(3), 4–18.

Moschkovich, J. (1999). Supporting the participation of English language learners in mathematical discussions. *For the Learning of Mathematics, 19*(1), 11–19.

[11] Informal communication with a teacher in Idaho Falls, Idaho, November 21, 2008.

[12] Social learning can be defined as a group of students discussing ideas and helping each other to learn.

[13] Fillmore, L.W. (1976). *The second time around: Cognitive and social strategies in second language acquisition.* Unpublished doctoral dissertation, Stanford University.

Moschkovich, J. (1999). Supporting the participation of English language learners in mathematical discussions. *For the Learning of Mathematics, 19*(1), 11–19.

Gibbons, P. (2002). *Scaffolding language scaffolding learning: Teaching second language learners in the mainstream classroom,* (pp. 6–10). Portsmouth, NH: Heinemann.

[14] Anstrom, K. (1999). *Preparing secondary education teachers to work with English language learners: Mathematics* (NCBE Resource Collection Series, No. 14). Washington, DC: National Clearinghouse for Bilingual Education.

[15] Buchanan, K., & Helman, M. (1997). *Reforming mathematics instruction for ESL literacy students.* Washington, DC: ERIC Clearinghouse on Languages and Linguistics.

Moschkovich, J. (1999). Supporting the participation of English language learners in mathematical discussions. *For the Learning of Mathematics, 19*(1), 11–19.

Cummins, J., & Swain, M. (1986). *Bilingualism in education: Aspects of theory, research and practice.* London: Longman.

[16] Ball, L., & Stacey, K. (n.d.). New literacies for mathematics: a new view of solving problems. Accessed January 14, 2009, from http://extranet.edfac.unimelb.edu.au/DSME/CAS-CAT/publicationsCASCAT/2001Pubspdf/BallStaceyNewLits.pdf.

[17] Bielenberg, B., & Fillmore, L.W. (Dec. 2004–Jan. 2005). The English they need for the test. *Educational Leadership, 62*(4), 45–49.

[18] Hawkins, B. (2005). Mathematics education for second language students in the mainstream classroom. In P.A. Richard-Amato, & M.A. Snow, (Eds.), *Academic success for English language learners*(p. 380). White Plains, NY: Pearson Education, Inc.

Bay-Williams, J.M., & Herrera, S. (2007). Is "just good teaching" enough to support the learning of English language learners? Insights from sociocultural learning theory. In W.G. Martin, M. E. Strutchens, & P.C. Elliott (Eds.), *The learning of mathematics: Sixty-ninth yearbook* (pp. 43–63). Reston, VA: National Council of Teachers of Mathematics.

Freeman, D.J. (2004). Teaching in the context of English-language learners: What we need to know. In M. Sadowski (Ed.), *Teaching immigrant and second-language students: Strategies for success* (pp. 7–20). Cambridge, MA: Harvard Education Press.

[19] National Research Council. (1999). *How people learn: Bridging research and practice*. Washington, DC: National Academies Press.

National Council of Teachers of Mathematics. (2000). *Principles and standards for school mathematics*. Reston, VA: Author.

Hawkins, B. (2005). Mathematics education for second language students in the mainstream classroom. In P.A. Richard-Amato, & M.A. Snow, (Eds.), *Academic success for English language learners*, (p. 380). White Plains, NY: Pearson Education, Inc.

[20] For example, mathematics curricula that use a similar structure are CME Project, Aim for Algebra, Connected Mathematics, IMP, Math Thematics, and UCSMP.

[21] The definitions of the three phases are loosely adapted from *Strategic Science Teaching for Grades K–12* (2002), a framework developed by the California County Superintendents Educational Services Association (CCSESA) Curriculum and Instruction Steering Committee (CISC) Science Subcommittee.

[22] Vang, C. (2004). Teaching science to English learners. *Language Magazine, 4*(4). Adapted with permission of *Language Magazine*, http://www.languagemagazine.com.

[23] Echevarria, J., Vogt, M., & Short, D.J. (2008). *Making content comprehensible for English learners: The SIOP® model* (3rd ed., pp. 131–132). Boston: Allyn & Bacon.

[24] Different states use different terms such as English Language Development (ELD), English Language Proficiency (ELP), or English as a Second Language (ESL) Standards.

[25] Bybee, R.W. (1997). *Achieving scientific literacy: From purposes to practices*. Portsmouth, NH: Heinemann.

[26] Krashen, S.D. (1985). *The input hypothesis: Issues and implications*. New York: Longman.

Krashen, S.D. (1981). *Second language acquisition and second language learning*. New York: Pergamon.

Long, M.H. (1981). Input, interaction, and second language acquisition. In H. Winitz (Ed.), *Native language and foreign language acquisition: Annals of the New York Academy of Science* (379, pp. 259–278).

[27] Wormeli, R. (2005). *Summarization in any subject* (p. 5). Alexandria, VA: Association for Supervision and Curriculum Development.

[28] Black, P., & William, D. (1998). Inside the black box: Raising standards through classroom assessment. *Phi Delta Kappan, 80*(2), 139–149. Accessed February 6, 2006, from http://www.pdkintl.org/kappan/kbla9810.htm.

[29] Cohen, E.G. (1994). *Designing groupwork: Strategies for the heterogeneous classroom*. New York: Teachers College Press.

[30] Boaler, J., & Humphreys, C. (2005). *Connecting mathematical ideas: Middle school video cases to support teaching and learning*. Portsmouth, NH: Heinemann.

[31] A number of sources inform this discussion of differentiating instruction. For example:

Cole, R.W. (Ed.). (1995). *Educating everybody's children: Diverse teaching strategies for diverse learners*; and Cole, R.W. (Ed.) (2001). *More strategies for educating everybody's children*. Alexandria, VA: Association for Supervision and Curriculum Development.

Gregory, G., & Chapman, C. (2001). *Differentiated instructional strategies: One size doesn't fit all*. Thousand Oaks, CA: Corwin Press.

Silver, H.F., Strong, R.W., & Perini, M.J. (2000). *So each may learn*. Alexandria, VA: Association for Supervision and Curriculum Development.

Tomlinson, C.A. (1999). *The differentiated classroom*. Alexandria, VA: Association for Supervision and Curriculum Development.

Tomlinson, C.A., & McTighe, J. (2006). *Integrating and differentiating instruction: Understanding by design*. Alexandria, VA: Association for Supervision and Curriculum Development.

CHAPTER 2

Understanding Language Development

Language is central to teaching and learning every subject. Teachers use language to help students learn content; students use language to explore content and to express what they have learned. Normally, children acquire a first language at home from their caregivers. By the time they reach school age, they have a good command of the basic sentence structures and vocabulary of their first language. However, for children learning a second language, there is much more variation. Depending on home, school, and community circumstances, some children quickly learn a second language to a native-like degree, whereas others learn the second language much more slowly. This chapter will explore theories of first and second language acquisition; the differences between social, or everyday, language and academic language; and implications for classroom instruction. Terms related to these discussions are defined in Figure 2.1.

FIRST LANGUAGE ACQUISITION

Most people have no memory of learning a first language; those who have learned a second language, on the other hand, usually remember at least some key aspects of the experience. This raises the question of whether first and second language acquisition are fundamentally similar or very different.

There are three major theories about how children acquire their first language: *behaviorist*; *innatist*; and *interactionist*.[1] This guidebook is based mostly in interactionist theory, which means, in part, that we encourage teachers to plan mathematics learning activities that involve teacher–student and student–student interactions within an inquiry-based approach to learning mathematics. Such an approach helps English learners acquire English as rapidly as possible, while they are investigating mathematical concepts and applications. Learning the academic language required to express mathematical thinking goes hand-in-hand with learning mathematics. Interactionist theory emphasizes the importance of learning in the context of interactions with fluent peers and adults. Teaching approaches based in this theory emphasize the benefits to English learners of listening to model speakers and practicing expressing their ideas, as they work together on authentic and structured mathematics activities. Acquiring a first language largely takes place during the first few years of life, so these theories of language acquisition have no direct implications for teaching in upper-grade classrooms. However, familiarity with these core concepts will help teachers understand the closely related theories of second language acquisition presented later in this chapter.

Behaviorist Theory

Behaviorists believe that children learn by receiving positive or negative reinforcement for their behaviors; these rewards and punishments then shape their future habits. For language acquisition, this would mean that children listen to spoken language in their environment and try to imitate the language they hear. When they produce correct forms, they would be praised, and when they produce incorrect forms, they would be corrected or misunderstood, resulting in the reinforcement of correct (or adult-like) use of language. Three predictions about language acquisition can be made based on behaviorist theory: (a) Children imitate what they hear. (b) Adults correct children to reinforce "correct" (adult) forms of language. (c) Children respond to the corrections by producing the correct forms. Each prediction can be tested by looking at the reality of first language acquisition.

Children imitate what they hear. This is true to a certain extent. Children do imitate quite a bit at certain phases of language acquisition, usually around age two to three years. However, young children rarely repeat exactly what they hear. They usually leave out transition words and repeat only content words. For example, a child hearing an adult say, "I'm going to the store now," might repeat this sentence as, "Going store now." It is unclear how children would learn the full set of sentence structures from getting reinforcement on these abbreviated sentences.

FIGURE 2.1. **Linguistic Terms**

Language. The word "language" in English describes two different concepts. The first is the abstract capacity humans have to represent thoughts, opinions, desires, and so forth in an external system that can be communicated to others (such as by sounds or signing). The second is the concrete, specific language used by a group of people, such as English, Spanish, Chinese, and American Sign Language. Another division is between direct and secondary representations of language. Speech and sign languages of the deaf (as developed by deaf people in a deaf cultural environment) represent the vocabulary and structures of language systems directly. Writing, as well as sign systems developed to represent a spoken language (such as signed English), are secondary since they represent spoken words and structures in another form.

Typically, young children learn direct language systems without formal instruction, by interacting with others in their environment, whereas they need specific instruction to learn secondary systems such as reading and writing. However, second language learners may need to learn both oral and written representations of their new language at the same time and may not be able to fully develop second language speech before starting to learn writing. Therefore, second language learners also may need explicit instruction in spoken language in order to accelerate all aspects of their language development.

Dialect. A dialect is a regional, social, or cultural variety of a wider language. Everyone speaks a dialect since everyone belongs to a particular regional, social, and cultural group at any given time. (In fact, each person has his or her own individual way of speaking — an idiolect.) The predominant dialect in a society is the one that becomes standardized in dictionaries and pedagogical grammar books, and this is called the "standard language." For example, standard English is the variety of English used by educated, middle-class speakers.

The standard language is often the variety that is considered to have "correct" grammar, while differences in the grammars of nonstandard varieties are considered "incorrect." However, this is simply a value judgment and does not reflect any underlying correctness in the system of that variety. Linguists have found that every language and every dialect spoken by human beings everywhere has a complete and rule-governed system.[2] Thus, from a linguistic point of view, there are no "primitive," "inadequate," or "bad" languages or dialects.

FIGURE 2.1. **Linguistic Terms (continued)**

Grammar. In linguistic terms, grammar is the system of rules for word formation, sentence structure, and pronunciation in a given language. Linguists develop descriptive grammars to describe the systematic rules underlying the languages or dialects they are studying. In schools, teachers tend to focus on prescriptive grammar rules — those that describe the structures of language that are considered proper or correct according to society, usually corresponding to the rules of the standard language in that society. Second language English learners will, of course, be taught standard English in school. However, teachers should be aware that students will also pick up elements of other varieties of English as they socialize with their peers.

First language. Also called native language, primary language, and mother tongue, the first language is the language a child learns at home from caregivers, usually between birth and age five. Children brought up in a bilingual environment may learn more than one first language. It is possible to learn a language in a native-like way until puberty.

Second language. A language learned after a first or native language has been acquired is called a second language. Though often used literally for a second consecutive language learned, this term encompasses any language or languages learned after any native language or languages. A second language can be learned after puberty, though speakers of a language learned at this stage will usually retain features that native speakers recognize as nonnative, such as differences in pronunciation (having an "accent") or certain grammatical structures.

Bilingual. Bilingual simply means "having two languages." Anyone who speaks more than one language is bilingual to some extent; however, this term is usually reserved for people who use two languages on a regular basis in everyday contexts. The terms "bilingual teaching" and "bilingual classrooms" refer to teaching methods or classrooms where two languages are used.

Source: Carr, J., Sexton, U., & Lagunoff, R. (2007). *Making Science Accessible to English Learners: A Guidebook for Teachers*. San Francisco, CA: WestEd.

Adults correct the form of children's language. This is true when children are older and already have a command of basic sentence structure. However, most often, especially with young children, adults respond to the content of the child's speech, rather than to the structure. Adults often respond as if they understand the child's approximations of language. For example, when a child points to an animal and says, "That cow," an adult might respond, "Yes, that's a cow," giving the child positive reinforcement for using an incorrect sentence structure, or, "No, that's a sheep," but not, "No, you must say, 'That is a cow.'"

Children respond to corrections by using correct forms. As children progress in their language learning, they typically go through a stage when they overgeneralize grammatical patterns and use structures adults never use, such as "I goed," or "two foots." While they are in this stage, no amount of adult correction or modeling has any effect. The children continue using these incorrect (but more regular) forms until the stage passes and they start using the irregular forms such as "went" and "feet." Thus, it appears children are figuring out these structures through some internal process and not from adult feedback.

Behaviorist theory can explain how children learn basic vocabulary and routine phrases (such as "bye-bye" or "thank you") but not how they learn complex sentence structure.

Innatist Theory

Proponents of the innatist theory reject the behaviorist explanation for language learning and posit that, instead of being a learned behavior, language seems to be acquired similarly to other innate skills, such as walking. All children are born with the capacity to acquire the skill of walking and, as they develop, they go through stages — crawling, standing, walking with support — that eventually lead to walking independently. Adults do not have to teach children how to walk by explaining the mechanism of walking or how to put one foot after the other — we assume children will learn to walk on their own, as long as their environment does not restrict or discourage them. Similarly, innatists believe children are born with the capacity to acquire language — they do not need to be taught language; instead, children innately go through stages that lead to speaking like an adult. Adults simply need to provide an environment in which children can figure out the rules of language on their own. Some of the central evidence for first language acquisition as an innate biological ability is summarized below.

Children experience uniform stages and attainment. All normally developing children go through similar stages of language acquisition at similar times, ultimately acquiring the basic vocabulary and sentence structures of the language(s) spoken with them. This is true across cultures, even when the environments are very different, and when caretakers interact with and speak to children in different ways.

First language must be acquired during a critical developmental period. Children in unusual circumstances who are not exposed to language before puberty do not appear able to learn adult-like language later in life. People learning a second language before puberty may be able to attain native ability to use a language, whereas people who learn a second language after puberty rarely attain native-level ability. As with some other biological functions, such as vision in humans, it appears that a first language must be acquired within a certain developmental period or it will be acquired only incompletely, if at all.

Children master the system of their first language without explicit evidence of all its possibilities. Children eventually learn the full system of their first language or dialect, even though they may not hear examples of all the specific language structures they eventually know and even though they are not instructed in or corrected about all the structures. In natural speaking, adults do not always use complete, well-flowing sentences. (A look at an unedited transcript of natural speech will show this.) They typically speak with fragments, false starts, unnoticed mistakes, repetitions, and unsignaled corrections of noticed mistakes. Children hear this natural speech without receiving explicit information about which parts are the incomplete, repeated, or uncorrected structures, and which are complete and correct. Thus, they must be starting out with some underlying knowledge about what language is and what the possible structures of human language are.

Innatist theory can be used to explain why a first language is learned without being taught. The details of the actual processes children go through and what underlying knowledge must be present in the mind for this to happen are still being studied.

Interactionist Theory

If exposure to adult language is all children need to learn their first language, then the question arises whether children need other people around to learn from or whether they could simply pick up their first language from TV or radio. There is strong evidence that children do not necessarily pick up a full system of language solely from passive exposure; it may be possible to learn some vocabulary and phrases in that way, but it appears that children learn how to produce complex forms by actually interacting with other speakers. The interactionist theory is based on this observation.

Proponents of the interactionist theory also point out that when adults or older children speak with younger children, they often automatically adjust their language, speaking more slowly and clearly, using simpler vocabulary and structures, and often repeating or paraphrasing. They also may respond to a young child's simple utterance with a grammatically complete adult version or an expansion. For example, if a child says, "Doggie sleeping," an adult might say, "Yes, the doggie is sleeping," or "The doggie is sleeping on the rug." While it is not clear that any particular interactive strategies are required to ensure a child learns language, the interactionist theory is built on the idea that some type of interactive communication is necessary for children to develop the full range of complex structures in a language.

Interactionist theory points to the environmental factors that must be present for children to learn language. When parties in a language interaction show what they do and do not understand, children are able to "test" and practice the system they are learning and try new or different ways to communicate.

SECOND LANGUAGE ACQUISITION

In the right circumstances, young children are able to successfully learn a second language without explicit instruction. On the other hand, adults typically need explicit instruction and much guided practice; even then, they often cannot attain native-like ability in a second language. Adolescents fall somewhere in between; while they may be able to pick up social language more quickly than adults, they may still need explicit instruction to become fully proficient in the grammar and academic language of their second language. The theories described below were originally developed as a means to explain incomplete second language acquisition among adults. With the increasing numbers of English learners in schools, these theories have been applied to second language learning among children and adolescents in the classroom as well. Some of these theories are directly related to the first language acquisition theories described previously.

Behaviorist Theory[3]

As noted, behaviorists believe that language learning takes places through repetition and reinforcement. Behaviorist theories of second language acquisition predict that second language learners will make mistakes in their second language based on the previously learned patterns in their first language. The main teaching method based on these theories, the audiolingual method, involves repetition drills (e.g., the teacher says a word or sentence and students repeat it), with a focus on getting learners to use correct pronunciation and grammar from the beginning. While this method results in adults being able to produce a series of learned phrases for a specific context, it does not give them a basis to communicate in an interactive way in other contexts.

Repetition and pattern drills can be very useful for teaching set phrases or new vocabulary, and they also are useful for helping shy students use oral language, since with choral repetition, chants, or songs they can speak along with a group instead of being singled out. However, for learning more complex structures and communicative abilities, other methods need to be used.

Creative Constructionist Theory[4]

This theory is based on the application of the innatist theory of first language acquisition to second language acquisition. Its best known proponent is Stephen Krashen, who developed a theory of second language learning consisting of five hypotheses.

First of all, the **acquisition-learning hypothesis** proposes that learning a second language is different from acquiring one. Learning involves conscious study of the forms of language, usually in a formal classroom environment, whereas acquiring a second language would be similar to what happens during first language acquisition — learners pick up language by hearing and using it, without any explicit instruction.

According to the **monitor hypothesis,** acquired language produces fluent usage and intuitive judgments about the correctness of language forms, whereas with learned language, a cognitive "monitor" must apply specific learned rules to speech or writing to make sure it is correct.

The **natural order hypothesis** states that rules of a language are acquired in a certain order, with some predictably acquired earlier and others later. This natural order is not affected by teaching. This hypothesis recalls the stages of first language acquisition.

In order to acquire language, learners must receive "comprehensible input." The **input hypothesis** states that comprehensible input is the combination of structures that the learner already knows, plus enough new structures so that the learner can still comprehend; this is written as "input plus one" or the formula $i + 1$. The input hypothesis holds that when the learner is exposed to new language in this way, it can then be acquired.

Finally, a learner's affective state can affect which input is acquired or not. The **affective filter hypothesis** states that when the "affective filter" is up — that is, when the learner feels anxious, self-conscious, or unmotivated — less acquisition will occur. When the filter is down and the learner feels relaxed and motivated, more acquisition will occur.

While Krashen's hypotheses are difficult to test and have not been proven empirically, they have intuitive appeal and have helped to move second language teaching away from grammar-book learning and toward more authentic, interactive methods.

The concept of comprehensible input has clear implications for the classroom, for native speakers and English speakers alike; while teachers should provide oral and written input to students near their proficiency level so they can comprehend the meaning, teachers should also provide some language, in context, just above students' proficiency level to help them acquire new language.

In addition, we know affective factors affect all types of learning; a fearful mind is closed to learning, while a relaxed mind is open to learning. As noted in the previous chapter, teachers who provide a respectful, caring classroom environment allow students to feel relaxed and to more readily learn language and content.

Interactionist Theory[5]

As with first language acquisition, interactionists believe that people learn a second language by interacting with native speakers in two-way conversations. In these language interactions, native speakers can be responsive to the needs of language learners by modifying their language with the explicit goal of making it comprehensible. Learners can negotiate their own comprehension by asking for clarification or repetition.

APPLICATIONS FOR ENGLISH LEARNERS

The more they get to interact with the teacher and classmates, the more opportunities second language learners will have to acquire language. Their language acquisition may be accelerated when the teacher provides rich, comprehensible input and encourages higher levels of language production. There are a number of ways teachers can modify their language to anticipate and address the needs of their English learners:

Comprehension checks. The teacher checks to see if the learner has understood (e.g., "The calculator must be put in your desk after use. What will you do with the calculator?").

Clarification requests. The teacher asks the learner to clarify a spoken communication (e.g., "Can you say that again?").

Repetition or paraphrase. The teacher repeats or restates an utterance (e.g., "Calculate the sine of a 25 degree angle. How can you use your calculator to find the sine?").

Nonverbal cues. The teacher supports utterances with visual cues such as gestures, written words, or pictures.

Corrective feedback. The teacher judiciously rephrases the learner's speech with correct forms within the flow of interactive conversation.

LANGUAGE AT SCHOOL: SOCIAL LANGUAGE AND ACADEMIC LANGUAGE

As noted above, all normally developing children in an interactive environment acquire the basic structures of their first language by the time they start school. Many second language learners will also be able to pick up the basics of a second language in this way — interacting with peers and hearing their new language used around them at school and in the community. It is important to realize, however, that literacy (reading and writing) and specific content area skills, including the vocabulary and structures used, must be explicitly taught in order for students to learn them. For many second language learners, this means learning both a new everyday, or social, language and a new academic language at the same time. Because these two types of language are learned in different ways, a student who is fluent in social language and can converse comfortably about people, places, and events is not necessarily fluent in academic language. Adolescent English learners with little or no prior schooling in their native countries may also be learning to read for the first time in any language.

Jim Cummins,[6] a well-known researcher of bilingualism, calls social language "basic interpersonal communicative skills" (BICS), and the language of literacy and academics "cognitive/academic language proficiency" (CALP). A theoretical model Cummins developed for understanding the difference between BICS and CALP is described in the following section. Full competency in BICS may take up to three years, and in CALP five to seven years.[7] Teachers should not assume that students must attain full fluency in BICS before advancing to content or learning activities requiring CALP.[8] Students can develop both BICS and CALP at the same time, especially since the boundary between BICS and CALP is not absolute — vocabulary and structures overlap, and spoken academic language is not usually formal and polished, except for prepared speeches.

Contextual Support and Cognitive Load

Figure 2.2 shows how communicative activities vary along two axes, "contextual support" and "cognitive load." Along the contextual support axis, "context-rich" communicative activities involve high levels of contextual support, such as voice intonation and gestures; "context-reduced" communicative activities involve low levels of contextual support, as is the case in telephone conversations or written notes or reports. On the cognitive load axis, cognitively "undemanding" activities require less thought or simultaneous processing; cognitively "demanding" activities require more thought or simultaneous processing. Thus, students may be able to quickly master BICS, that is, be able to effectively interact in their second language in quadrant A — in cognitively undemanding situations where there are many contextual supports, such as a conversation with peers on the playground. However, students may take much longer to master CALP, which requires them to interact effectively in their second language in quadrant D, in cognitively demanding situations with few contextual supports, such as reading word problems on their own or listening to a long academic lecture.[9] Students learning new vocabulary and language forms at the same time they're learning new mathematics concepts experience a higher cognitive load than students who are proficient in English and need only concentrate on the new mathematics concepts. This high cognitive load is one reason why teachers need to pause frequently during direct instruction, allowing time for English learners to cognitively process both the English and the mathematics.

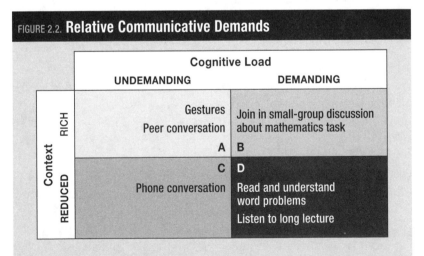

FIGURE 2.2. **Relative Communicative Demands**

	Cognitive Load	
	UNDEMANDING	DEMANDING
Context RICH	Gestures Peer conversation A	Join in small-group discussion about mathematics task B
Context REDUCED	C Phone conversation	D Read and understand word problems Listen to long lecture

Source: Carr, J., Sexton, U., & Lagunoff, R. (2007). *Making Science Accessible to English Learners: A Guidebook for Teachers*. San Francisco, CA: WestEd.

Three major implications of the BICS/CALP theory apply to the instruction of English learners. The first is that teachers should not assume that students' fluency in everyday English is a sign of equal proficiency in using and understanding English for academic purposes. For example, a student may be able to converse easily with peers and with the teacher in one-to-one, face-to-face situations but may not as easily understand a lecture or a video presentation.

The second implication is that teachers can make academic content more accessible to English learners by providing more contextual cues to guide student learning, such as connecting new lessons to students' prior knowledge, planning hands-on and interactive learning activities, and using pictures and graphic organizers. These contextual cues should be varied in order to tap into students' strengths in diverse learning modes such as auditory, visual, spatial, and kinesthetic. Providing cues and visuals, and connecting what students will learn to what they already know, enriches the context and lowers the cognitive load.

The third implication is that teachers should carefully consider when to focus on correcting a student's language forms, versus when to focus on whether the student understands the content. When students are involved in cognitively undemanding activities, they will be able to turn their attention to self-correction or teacher correction (revoicing with substitutions) of vocabulary choice and language forms. When they are involved in cognitively demanding activities, corrections will be a distraction and will impose an even higher cognitive load.

The suggestions in this chapter for working with English learners reflect the extra challenge students learning a second language face, compared to that of acquiring a first language. They also take into account the increased cognitive load of learning academic language, compared to that of learning or acquiring social language. A summary of these suggestions appears in Figure 2.3.

FIGURE 2.3. Teaching Tips That Reflect Language Acquisition Theory

» Use drills, choral repetition, chants, or songs for practicing new vocabulary and phrases. For example, a song or chant could be used to practice naming polygons, identifying classes of numbers, or labeling parts of a graph.

» When presenting information orally, repeat, rephrase, and expand on terms and structures; refer to related visual scaffolds when possible.

» Check for comprehension by asking open-ended questions to assess a student's understanding ("What happens when…?") rather than yes-no questions ("Did you understand?").

» Show respect towards students and toward their first language and home culture. Build on their previous knowledge. Let students know they will not be ridiculed for making mistakes. Give them positive reasons to learn mathematics and communicate in English.

» Make sure all students have opportunities to communicate both with one another and with the teacher. Vary the classroom organization among individual, pair, small group, and whole group work.

» Provide a variety of contextual cues when explaining new or abstract content. Connect ideas to students' previous experiences; involve them in hands-on activities; use pictures, graphics, and graphic organizers to support written and spoken information.

» Provide information and activities in different learning modes: auditory, visual, spatial, and kinesthetic.

» Choose carefully when to focus on correcting language forms. The best time for focusing on form is when students are involved in less cognitively demanding activities. Let them know in advance that form will be a focus. Focus on those forms that interfere with meaning, rather than minor details.

Source: Carr, J., Sexton, U., & Lagunoff, R. (2007). *Making Science Accessible to English Learners: A Guidebook for Teachers*. San Francisco, CA: WestEd.

ENDNOTES FOR CHAPTER 2

[1] The sections of this chapter on first and second language acquisition are based on the overall conceptual organization of parts of Lightbown, P.M., & Spada, N. (1993). *How languages are learned*. Oxford: Oxford University Press.

[2] One exception is *pidgins*, which arise when people who speak different languages must communicate with each other yet do not have the time or desire to learn one another's language. The result is a simple word-based system without complex grammar. What is interesting is that in the next generation, speakers develop a more complex system from the pidgin, and this new variety is now a complete language in its own right.

[3] Lado, R. (1964). *Language teaching: A scientific approach*. New York: McGraw-Hill.

[4] Dulay, H., Burt, M., & Krashen, S. (1982). *Language two*. Oxford: Oxford University Press.

Krashen, S. (1982). *Principles and practice in second language acquisition*. Oxford: Pergamon.

[5] Long, M. H. (1985). Input and second language acquisition theory. In S. Gass & C. Madden (Eds.), *Input in second language acquisition* (pp. 377–393). Rowley, MA: Newbury House.

[6] Cummins, J. (1979). Cognitive/academic language proficiency, linguistic interdependence, the optimum age question and some other matters. *Working Papers on Bilingualism, 19*, 121–129.

[7] Hakuta, K., Goto Butler, Y., & Witt, D. (2000). How long does it take English learners to attain proficiency? *University of California Linguistic Minority Research Institute, Policy Report 2000–1*. Accessed April 18, 2006, from http://faculty.ucmerced.edu/khakuta/research/publications.html.

[8] Marzano, R.J., & Pickering, D.J. (2005). *Building academic vocabulary teacher's manual*. Alexandria, VA: Association for Supervision and Curriculum Development.

[9] For more information on cognitive demand in mathematics, see:

Smith, M. S., & Stein, M. K. (1998, February). Selecting and creating mathematical tasks: From research to practice. *Mathematics Teaching in the Middle School, 3*, 344–350.

Arbaugh, F., & Brown, C. A. (2004). What makes a mathematical task worthwhile? Designing a learning tool for high school mathematics teachers. In R. N. Rubenstein & G. W. Bright (Eds.), *Perspectives on the teaching of mathematics: Sixty-sixth yearbook* (pp. 27–41). Reston, VA: National Council of Teachers of Mathematics.

CHAPTER 3

Understanding Five Levels of English Language Development

People do not learn either a first or second language all at once, but in stages—gradually increasing the use and comprehension of vocabulary and grammatical structures over time. This chapter addresses the stages, or levels, of second language acquisition, with a focus on academic language. In the upper elementary and secondary grades, the levels assume literacy in a first language, but this may not be the case for individual students, of course. Teachers will want a clear understanding of each English learner's previous academic experience and current English language development (ELD) level in order to best support content learning, appropriately assess what a student knows, and use that feedback to tailor instruction.

> **5 ELD Levels**
> Beginning
> Early Intermediate
> Intermediate
> Early Advanced
> Advanced

For this chapter, the authors Carr, Lagunoff, and Sexton created a set of charts (Figures 3.1, 3.2, and 3.3, and Appendix B) that teachers can use to quickly see which academic language skills can be expected at five ELD levels, judge their own English learners' current proficiency levels, and consider instructional strategies appropriate to each ELD level. The charts help teachers plan differentiated lessons for teaching and assessing students within their general levels of English language development.

The five levels—*beginning, early intermediate, intermediate, early advanced,* and *advanced*—represent distinctions often made in ELD standards. States differ in terminology; for instance, some states use the term ELP (for English language proficiency) and refer to performance indicators or benchmarks instead of standards. Title III of the federal No Child Left Behind Act refers to the five ELD/ELP levels and the labels used in this guidebook.

Figure 3.1 shows five levels of English language development and very general student language behaviors at each level, along with teacher strategies appropriate to a given level. Figures 3.2 and 3.3 show more specific academic language skills (ALS) at each level, for grades 6–8 and grades 9–12, respectively. (Appendix B contains ALS charts for grades K–2 and 3–5.) The descriptors at each ELD level reflect mastery of that level. A newly arrived English learner who understands few or no words in English is working in the *beginning* level but is far from representing mastery of those descriptors. Knowing what to expect of English learners at the different ELD levels helps a teacher plan instruction that ensures that English learners can access the curriculum.

As we noted in chapter 2, it may take five to seven years for an English learner to achieve academic language proficiency close to that of a native English speaker (reading and writing proficiency, as well as listening and speaking proficiency). English learners, like other students, are very heterogeneous, and their progress can depend on a complexity of factors, so individuals may reach proficiency in less than five years or more than seven years. This level of native-like academic language proficiency is represented by the *early advanced* or *advanced* levels in the ALS charts. Mathematics teachers may have English learners in their classrooms who are at some or all of the five levels, and any individual student's skill level may vary, depending on whether a listening, speaking, reading, or writing skill is being assessed. Also, native English speakers in the classroom who struggle with reading and writing skills may not be proficient in academic English and may exemplify descriptors in lower levels of the ALS charts.

The mathematics teacher has the challenge of teaching grade-level mathematics concepts within a year to students who take many years to reach academic English proficiency. The high school English learner cannot wait five years to learn high school mathematics. So the mathematics teacher must support English communication during instruction, so that English learners have the opportunity to focus on the mathematics content. Using a variety of the scaffolding strategies that are described throughout the remaining chapters of this guidebook is a good place to start.

For assessment purposes, the ALS charts that follow can be used as rubrics to judge the proficiency level of an English learner at any point in time. Often the only assessment data available to teachers are state test scores, which may be both too general and months too old to help guide instruction. The charts contain what we consider to be the essential academic language skills for instruction and assessment in any content area. Figure 3.1 presents expectations for student language performance and a list of teaching strategies for each language level, and Figures 3.2 and 3.3 present the ALS charts that teachers can use to plan instruction according to the levels of English language skills in their classrooms for grades six through eight and nine through 12, respectively.

FIGURE 3.1. Student and Teacher Behaviors at Five ELD Levels

Level	Expected Student Performance	Teacher Strategies
Beginning	Understand brief, very basic, highly contextualized input with visual support. Respond to simple social talk and academic instruction by using gestures or a few words, phrases, and simple subject-verb-object sentences. Read very brief text with simple sentence forms and mostly familiar vocabulary. Exhibit many errors of convention (grammar, pronunciation, written mechanics).	Use target vocabulary and sentence structure based on student's comprehension; repeat and rephrase; accompany oral instruction with visuals and hands-on activities. Make connections to student's prior personal and academic experiences. Ask basic, factual questions that can be answered with gestures or a few words. Address various learning modalities. Categorize learned words on wall charts, by concept, for easy reference. Use brief texts with pictures at student's readability level. Provide mostly completed chapter outlines with a few blanks for student to complete. Scaffold writing (such as with models, sentence frames). Assess student orally and perhaps use Cloze sentences and labeled graphic organizers.
Early Intermediate	Understand brief, basic, contextualized input with visual supports. Respond with increasing ease to a greater variety of social and academic communication tasks. Respond by using phrases and simple sentences, more target vocabulary. Read text with simple sentence structures and mostly familiar vocabulary. Exhibit many errors of convention.	Use vocabulary and sentence structure based on student's comprehension; repeat and rephrase; accompany oral instruction with visuals and hands-on activities. Make connections to student's prior personal and academic experiences. Ask fairly basic, factual questions that can be answered with a few words or simple phrases. Address various learning modalities. Categorize learned words on wall charts, by concept, for easy reference. Use texts with pictures at student's readability level. Provide partially completed chapter outlines with about 8–12 blanks for student to complete. Scaffold writing (such as with models, sentence frames). Assess student using graphic organizers and moderately supportive sentence frames.

FIGURE 3.1. **Student and Teacher Behaviors at Five ELD Levels (continued)**

Level	Expected Student Performance	Teacher Strategies
Intermediate	Understand and be understood in many basic social situations. Understand more complex input, but still need contextual and visual support in academic language. Respond by using expanded vocabulary and connected, expanded sentences. Apply the English language skills that have been taught to meet immediate communication and learning needs. Read text with mostly familiar vocabulary or participate in small group reading of texts. Exhibit many errors of convention.	Choose vocabulary and sentence structure based on student's comprehension; repeat and rephrase as needed; accompany oral instruction with visuals and hands-on activities. Make connections to student's prior personal and academic experiences. Ask critical thinking questions that can be answered with phrases and simple sentences. Address various learning modalities. Provide texts at student's readability level. Teach student to use glossaries and his or her vocabulary notes as references. Provide models and less scaffolding for writing. Assess student using sentence frames/starters; follow with specific oral prompting for ambiguities.
Early Advanced	Understand complex input appropriate for the grade level with some need for visual supports. Respond by using expanded vocabulary in expanded sentences. Combine the elements of the English language in complex, cognitively demanding social and academic situations. Read grade-level texts with preview of content and key words. Exhibit some minor errors of convention.	Use vocabulary and sentence structure normal for grade level. Make connections to student's prior learning. Ask critical thinking questions and encourage responses that are detailed sentences. Address various learning modalities. Provide texts at student's readability level and grade level. Provide models and minimal use of scaffolds for writing; integrate language arts and content-area activities and give feedback to continue developing language and writing skills. Assess student's independent writing; provide clear directions, writing models, and paragraph starters/outline.
Advanced	Fully understand input appropriate for the grade level. Respond with expanded vocabulary and connected, expanded sentences. Communicate effectively with various audiences on a range of familiar and new topics to meet social and academic demands; may need further linguistic enhancement and refinement to reach the level of native language peers. Read grade-level texts independently.	Use vocabulary and sentence structure normal for grade level. Make connections to student's prior learning. Ask critical thinking questions and encourage responses that are detailed sentences. Address various learning modalities. Provide texts at student's grade level. Writing may need minimal use of scaffolds; integrate language arts and content-area activities and give feedback to continue developing language and writing skills. Assess student's independent writing; provide clear directions.

Source: Carr, J., Sexton, U., & Lagunoff, R. (2007). *Making Science Accessible to English Learners: A Guidebook for Teachers*. San Francisco, CA: WestEd.

FIGURE 3.2. Academic Language Skills Grades 6–8

Skill	Beginning	Early Intermediate	Intermediate	Early Advanced	Advanced
Listen with Comprehension	Listen to and follow simple directions. Listen to teacher's simple questions, answers, and brief explanations aided by appropriate scaffolds. Show understanding by identifying one or a few key ideas using gestures and phrases.	Listen to and follow more complex directions. Listen to teacher's questions, answers, and brief explanations aided by appropriate scaffolds. Show understanding by identifying some key ideas using simple sentences.	Listen to and follow multi-step directions. Listen to teacher's questions, answers, and explanations aided by appropriate scaffolds. Show understanding by describing key ideas using complete sentences with more details.	Listen to and follow multi-step directions. Listen during teacher's lesson and engage in class discussion with visual aids. Show understanding by explaining key ideas using detailed sentences.	Same as early advanced.
Use Academic Vocabulary	Use basic social vocabulary and a few academic vocabulary words in simple phrases and sentences to communicate basic meaning in social and academic settings.	Use some academic vocabulary words in sentences to communicate meaning. Use context clues to understand a few unknown words.	Use expanded academic vocabulary in more detailed sentences to express ideas. Use glossary, knowledge of word parts, and context to understand some unknown words. Recognize multiple meanings of some words.	Use expanded academic vocabulary in detailed sentences to express complex ideas. Use knowledge of word parts and context as well as dictionary to understand unknown words. Recognize multiple meanings of many words.	Same as early advanced.
Ask and Answer Questions	Orally ask and answer simple factual comprehension questions about listening or reading passages using simple phrases and sentences.	Orally ask and answer factual comprehension questions about listening or reading passages using simple sentences.	Ask and answer factual and simple inferential comprehension questions about listening or reading passages using some detailed sentences.	Ask and answer factual and inferential comprehension questions about listening or reading passages using detailed sentences.	Same as early advanced.

FIGURE 3.2. **Academic Language Skills Grades 6–8 (continued)**

Skill	Beginning	Early Intermediate	Intermediate	Early Advanced	Advanced
Explain Main Ideas	Orally identify a main idea and a few details in a listening or reading passage using phrases and simple sentences.	Orally describe a main idea and some important details in a listening or reading passage using simple sentences.	Orally or in writing, explain the main ideas in a listening or reading passage by connecting to some important details.	Orally or in writing, explain the main ideas in a listening or reading passage by connecting to important details.	Orally or in writing, explain the main ideas in a listening or reading passage by connecting to important details and using expanded vocabulary.
Use Writing Strategies	Organize and record information by displaying it in pictures, lists, charts, and tables.	Collect information from various sources, take basic notes, and write and revise a brief paragraph by following an outline.	Use strategies of basic note taking, outlining, and revising to structure drafts of simple essays or reports.	Use strategies of note taking, outlining, summarizing, and revising to structure drafts of mostly clear, coherent, and focused essays or reports.	Use strategies of note taking, outlining, summarizing, and revising to structure drafts of clear, coherent, and focused essays or reports.
Write Compositions	Create phrases and simple sentences. Write brief compositions that have a main idea. Exhibit many major errors of language conventions.	Write brief, simple compositions that include a main idea and some details. Exhibit many major errors of language conventions.	Write brief compositions that include a thesis and some supporting details. Exhibit few major and some minor errors of language conventions.	Write compositions that include a clear thesis and supporting details. Exhibit some minor errors of language conventions.	Write well-developed compositions that include a clear thesis and supporting details. Exhibit few, minor errors of language conventions.
Write Research Reports	Gather basic information as part of a group. Present information graphically with labels and write simple sentences. Exhibit many major errors of language conventions.	Gather more complex information as part of a group. Present information graphically and write brief summary paragraphs. Exhibit many major errors of language conventions.	Investigate a topic as part of a group. Develop a brief report that includes source citations. Exhibit few major and some minor errors of language conventions.	Investigate a topic and write a full report that conveys information; use technical terms, citations, and a bibliography. Exhibit some minor errors of language conventions.	Investigate and write reports that clarify and defend positions with evidence and logical reasoning; use technical terms, citations, and a bibliography. Exhibit few, minor errors of language conventions.

FIGURE 3.2. **Academic Language Skills Grades 6–8 (continued)**

Skill	Beginning	Early Intermediate	Intermediate	Early Advanced	Advanced
Communicate Critical Thinking	Compare and contrast. Identify cause and effect and sequential order relationships. Identify facts and opinions. Form basic hypotheses and conclusions.	Compare and contrast. Identify cause and effect and sequential order relationships. Distinguish between fact and opinion. Hypothesize and conclude.	Compare and contrast. Describe cause and effect and sequential order relationships. Distinguish between fact and opinion. Hypothesize, infer, generalize, and conclude.	Compare and contrast. Analyze cause and effect and sequential order relationships. Distinguish among fact, opinion, and supported inferences. Hypothesize, infer, generalize, and conclude.	Compare and contrast. Analyze cause and effect and sequential order relationships. Identify relative credibility of information. Hypothesize, infer, generalize, and conclude.

Source: Carr, J., Sexton, U., & Lagunoff, R. (2007). *Making Science Accessible to English Learners: A Guidebook for Teachers*. San Francisco, CA: WestEd.

FIGURE 3.3. Academic Language Skills Grades 9–12

Skill	Beginning	Early Intermediate	Intermediate	Early Advanced	Advanced
Listen with Comprehension	Listen to and follow simple directions. Listen to teacher's simple questions, answers, and brief explanations aided by appropriate scaffolds. Show understanding by identifying one or a few key ideas using gestures and phrases.	Listen to and follow more complex directions. Listen to teacher's questions, answers, and brief explanations aided by appropriate scaffolds. Show understanding by identifying some key ideas using simple sentences.	Listen to and follow multi-step directions. Listen to teacher's questions, answers, and explanations aided by appropriate scaffolds. Show understanding by describing key ideas using complete sentences with more details.	Listen to and follow multi-step directions. Listen during teacher's lesson and engage in class discussion with visual aids. Show understanding by explaining key ideas using detailed sentences.	Same as early advanced.
Use Academic Vocabulary	Use basic social vocabulary and a few academic vocabulary words in simple phrases and sentences to communicate basic meaning in social and academic settings.	Use some academic vocabulary words in sentences to communicate meaning. Use context clues to understand a few unknown words.	Use expanded academic vocabulary in more detailed sentences to express ideas. Use glossary, knowledge of word parts, and context to understand some unknown words. Recognize multiple meanings of some words.	Use expanded academic vocabulary in detailed sentences to express complex ideas. Use knowledge of word parts and context as well as dictionary to understand unknown words. Recognize multiple meanings of many words.	Same as early advanced.
Ask and Answer Questions	Orally ask and answer simple factual comprehension questions about listening or reading passages using simple phrases and sentences.	Orally ask and answer factual comprehension questions about listening or reading passages using simple sentences.	Ask and answer factual and simple inferential comprehension questions about listening or reading passages using some detailed sentences.	Ask and answer factual and inferential comprehension questions about listening or reading passages using detailed sentences.	Same as early advanced.

FIGURE 3.3. **Academic Language Skills Grades 9–12 (continued)**

Skill	Beginning	Early Intermediate	Intermediate	Early Advanced	Advanced
Analyze Main Ideas	Orally identify a main idea and a few details of a listening or reading passage using phrases and simple sentences.	Orally describe a main idea and some important details in a listening or reading passage using simple sentences.	Orally or in writing, explain the main ideas in a listening or reading passage by connecting to important details.	Orally or in writing, analyze the main ideas in a listening or reading passage by connecting to important details and using expanded vocabulary.	Same as early advanced.
Use Writing Strategies	Organize and record information by displaying it in pictures, lists, charts, and tables.	Collect information from various sources, take basic notes, and write and revise a brief paragraph by following an outline.	Use strategies of basic note taking, outlining, and revising to structure drafts of simple essays or reports.	Use strategies of note taking, outlining, summarizing, and revising to structure drafts of mostly clear, coherent, and focused essays or reports.	Use strategies of note taking, outlining, summarizing, and revising to structure drafts of clear, coherent, and focused essays or reports.
Write Compositions	Create phrases and simple sentences. Write brief compositions that have a main idea. Exhibit many major errors of language conventions.	Write brief, simple compositions that include a main idea and some details. Exhibit many major errors of language conventions.	Write brief compositions that include a thesis and some points of support. Exhibit a few major and some minor errors of language conventions.	Write compositions that include a clear thesis and describe organized points of support. Exhibit some minor errors of language conventions.	Write compositions that provide evidence in support of a thesis and related claims and counter-arguments. Exhibit few, minor errors of language conventions.

FIGURE 3.3. **Academic Language Skills Grades 9–12 (continued)**

Skill	Beginning	Early Intermediate	Intermediate	Early Advanced	Advanced
Write Research Reports	Gather basic information as part of a group. Present information graphically with labels and write simple sentences. Exhibit many major errors of language conventions.	Gather more complex information as part of a group. Present information graphically and write brief summary paragraphs. Exhibit many major errors of language conventions.	Investigate a topic as part of a group. Develop brief reports that include source citations. Exhibit few major and some minor errors of language conventions.	Investigate a topic and write full reports that convey information; use technical terms, citations, and a bibliography. Use academic language. Exhibit some minor errors of language conventions.	Investigate and write reports that clarify and defend positions with evidence and logical reasoning; use technical terms, citations, and a bibliography. Use academic language. Exhibit few, minor errors of language conventions.
Communicate Critical Thinking	Compare and contrast. Identify cause and effect and sequential order relationships. Identify facts and opinions. Form basic hypotheses and conclusions.	Compare and contrast. Identify cause and effect and sequential order relationships. Distinguish between fact and opinion. Hypothesize and conclude.	Compare and contrast. Analyze cause and effect and sequential order relationships. Distinguish among fact, opinion, and supported inferences. Hypothesize, infer, generalize, and conclude.	Same as intermediate.	Compare and contrast. Analyze cause and effect and sequential order relationships. Identify relative credibility of factual information. Hypothesize, infer, generalize, and conclude.

Source: Carr, J., Sexton, U., & Lagunoff, R. (2007). *Making Science Accessible to English Learners: A Guidebook for Teachers*. San Francisco, CA: WestEd.

CHAPTER 4

Teaching the Language of Mathematics

In mathematics, much of what students need to learn requires that they master specialized vocabulary and discipline-specific ways of using language, whether for listening, speaking, reading, or writing. Integrating language instruction into content instruction is a research-based approach that works, and effective mathematics teachers do this for all their students.[1] Integrating language and content instruction accelerates English language development, shortens the delay before English learners have equitable access to content curriculum, and supports culturally and linguistically inclusive classrooms.[2] For students who also are English learners, learning language in the context of learning mathematics is not simply beneficial, it is crucial.[3] Language learning and content learning are inseparable — and reciprocal.[4]

This chapter describes the teacher's role in facilitating students' language use and presents some concrete steps for teaching new vocabulary. Then a number of tools are introduced that the mathematics teacher can use to help students organize mathematics concepts and vocabulary.

THE LEXICON AND DISCOURSE OF MATHEMATICS

Academic language that relates specifically to mathematics is the *lexicon of mathematics* — the set of terms mathematicians and mathematics learners use to communicate about their subject matter. These content words and phrases have a specific meaning in the context of the discipline. For example, "quadratic," "algebraic," "quotient," and "square root" have specific meanings in mathematics and are clearly part of the lexicon of mathematics. Some of these content words, such as "formula," are used in place of everyday words,

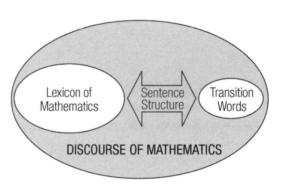

such as "rule," as illustrated in Figure 4.1. On the other hand, some everyday words have a specific meaning in a mathematics context (e.g., "positive," "negative," "table," "rational," "irrational"). Finally, in some cases several words can describe one specific mathematical operation (e.g., "add," "plus," "sum," "combine").[5]

While some terms are exclusive to mathematics, others overlap disciplines. For example, such mathematical terms as "difference" and "evaluate" have different meanings in other disciplines. "Difference" means the answer to a subtraction operation in mathematics, but, in science, it refers to a quality that is not the same about two items. In mathematics, "to evaluate an equation" means to find the values that make the equation true. In the social sciences, "to evaluate a source" means to rate the quality of the source. Teachers in different disciplines who share a set of students may want to identify an interdisciplinary lexicon and coordinate vocabulary instruction so students easily see a word's meaning connections and discern any shades of meaning particular to a discipline.

FIGURE 4.1. Interdisciplinary Terms	
EVERYDAY WORD	**MATHEMATICAL LANGUAGE**
Guess	Estimate, Conjecture
Rule	Axiom, Property, Formula
Same	Equal, Congruent, Equivalent
Take Away	Subtract, Difference

When this vocabulary is used in sentences, further comprehension challenges arise. National Council of Teachers of Mathematics (NCTM) standards[6] and research on the language of mathematics[7] point out that mathematics discourse patterns and syntactical structures can be daunting for English learners to understand and use. Active voice sentences tend to be easier to comprehend than passive voice sentences, but passive voice is often used in mathematics-related text and speech (e.g., ten [is] divided by two). Moreover, mathematics textbooks usually lack the redundancy or paraphrasing that assists English learners to understand the text.

A mathematics statement can be expressed entirely in symbols or in very technical language. In regard to symbolic vocabulary, consider the very different, abstract meaning of the numeral 2 in the following contexts: 52, 23, 4^2, 1/2, 2/3 and 2n.[8] In the United States, the symbol 5^2 can be read as "5 squared," "5 to the second power," or "5 to the second."[9] Often, there is not direct correspondence between how symbols and words are ordered (e.g., "a is five less than b" means $a = b - 5$, not $a = 5 - b$).[10] English learners who try to translate word-for-word may have difficulty interpreting the meaning of logical connectors, such as "if," "because," and "however."[11] In addition, within mathematics, notational and procedural differences exist between the United States and other countries. Figure 4.2 illustrates key mathematical differences between the U.S. and Latin American countries.

Transition words and phrases are the necessary connectors for relating mathematical ideas and signaling their organization. These words and phrases do not refer to anything in and of themselves, but they have important roles — to signal grammatical, logical, or rhetorical relationships. "Because," "for example," and "in order to" are some common transition words or phrases. English learners may not be aware that fairly common transition words can be applied differently in different disciplines. For example, the transition word "by" has many meanings, depending on context, such as "by the river" in literature, "by 1803" in social science, "multiply 3 by 4" in mathematics, and "by osmosis" in science. Native English speakers learn these terms as a matter of course. For English learners, a special effort must be made to help them master them.

Figure 4.3 lists commonly used transition words and phrases that English learners need to understand.

FIGURE 4.2. Mathematical Notational and Procedural Comparisons Between U.S. and Latin American Countries

	United States	Latin American Countries
Reading Numbers	Numbers with 10, 11, or 12 digits are designated as billions. 8,000,000,000 is read "eight billion" 8,000,000,000,000 is read "eight trillion"	Numbers with at least 13 digits are designated as billions. 8,000,000,000 is read "eight thousand million" 8,000,000,000,000 is read "eight billion"
Separation of digits in large numbers	Comma	Decimal point, space, comma, apostrophe, or semicolon
Negative Numbers	Preceding negative sign (–)	Preceding negative sign (–) or bar over the number
Repeating Decimals	Bar over repeating digits or ellipsis following digits 0.32 = 0.3232…	Arc over repeating digits 0.32
Decimal Fractions	Decimal point 4.56	Comma 4,56
Operation Symbols	Colon denotes division primarily in ratios.	Colon is one of four symbols denoting division.
Angle Notation	Angle symbol to the left of angle name	Angle symbol above angle name
Measurement	US Customary	Metric
Prime Factorization	Factor Tree	Vertical Line
Division of Fractions	Invert second fraction and then multiply	Cross-multiply
Least Common Multiple	Use prime factorization	Multiply common prime factors and the prime factors that appear in each number
Subtraction Algorithm	Renaming method $42 - 19 = (30 + 12) - (10 + 9)$	"Equal additions" method $42 - 19 = (40 + 2) - (10 + 9)$ $= (40 + 12) - (20 + 9)$
Division Algorithm	"Long" division	Rely more on mental mathematics or "short" division
Parentheses	Evaluate within parentheses first	Use distributive property
Algebraic Equations	Perform operations on both expressions of the equation $x + 35 = 75$ $x + 35 - 35 = 75 - 35$ $x = 40$	Mentally find missing number in each operation $x + 35 = 75$ What plus 35 equals 75? $40 + 35 = 75$

Source: Adapted from Perkins, I., & Flores, A. (2002). Mathematical notations and procedures of recent immigrant students. *Mathematics Teaching in the Middle School, 7,* 346–351. Reston, VA: National Council of Teachers of Mathematics (NCTM), with permission from NCTM and TODOS.

FIGURE 4.3. **Common Transition Words**

Many transition words or phrases can be used as Sentences Starters, while some connect ideas inside a sentence. They can be provided to English learners on posters to support oral language and in sentence frames to support written communication.

Purpose	Transition Words			
Giving a definition	is equal to	means	refers to	is synonymous with
	is the same as	in other words	consists of	in fact
Providing an example	for example	for instance	such as	is like
	including	to illustrate		
Suggesting more ideas	furthermore	also finally	another	moreover
Sequencing	first…second	next	initially	before
	preceding	when	finally	after
	following	as	not long after	now
Comparing	same as	just like/as	in the same way	in comparison
	not only…but also	as well as	similarly	
Contrasting	different from	as opposed to	instead of	in contrast
	however	but	although	yet
	while	on the other hand		
Showing cause and effect relationships	because	as a result of	may be due to	since
	consequently	this led to	so that	nevertheless
	in order to	effects of	for this reason	if … then
	therefore	thus		
Describing problems and solutions	one answer is	one reason is	a solution is	the problem is
	the question is			
Expressing an opinion or conclusion	I think	I believe that	I predict that	I suggest that
	I conclude that	I deduce that	I speculate that	in my opinion
	I agree with ____ that			
Reporting findings or outcomes	I/We found that	I/We learned that	I/We discovered that	I/We observed that

Source: Adapted with permission from English Learners and the Language Arts (ELLA). (2003). San Francisco: WestEd.

To use the lexicon of mathematics, English learners need to practice using it in sentences and extended discourse. Sentence structure governs the formation of sentences — the combining of content and transition words into statements, questions, and commands.

At a level beyond the sentence, discourse involves use of language to convey extended expression of thought on a topic in connected speech or writing. A key aspect of the discourse of mathematicians is communication about the procedures of mathematics — for example, knowing how to provide a solution supported by mathematical reasoning; how to write a summary or explanation of a mathematics investigation; or how to present arguments for a mathematical conclusion and how to write a mathematical proof. John Mason[12] describes a simple way to help adolescents (English learners as well as native English speakers) understand the importance of convincing explanations. You can convince yourself, convince a friend, or convince a skeptic. Mathematics values explanations that will convince a skeptic using clear, precise language and based on fact and logic.

FACILITATING STUDENTS' LANGUAGE USE

English learners at different developmental levels can all learn the lexicon and discourse of mathematics. However, as we saw in chapters 2 and 3, the complexity of these language components will vary according to students' English proficiency. One way to think about this is that all students will learn the same mathematics concepts, but the teacher will need to adjust the complexity of language he or she uses to explain these concepts depending on each student's English proficiency level.

In addition to adjusting and differentiating language for learners at different stages of English proficiency, the teacher also supports English learners (as well as visual and kinesthetic learners) with hands-on activities and visuals. Visuals might be real objects, pictures, illustrations, graphic organizers, word walls, or board notes.

The teacher repeats and rephrases for English learners, and provides adequate wait time (five to seven seconds) before asking for responses to provide English learners and other students who need more time to process information, access to the discussion. As noted in chapter 1, wait time encourages deeper thinking and equalizes students' opportunities to respond.

When providing corrective feedback to English learners, the mathematics teacher focuses first on ideas and meaning, especially when the student is struggling to communicate complex concepts. In these cognitively demanding situations, the teacher might simply ignore grammar errors. Feedback in these instances takes the form of "mathematical rephrasing" to help students understand how to express their mathematical ideas in English. For example, the English learner says, "I [looks at the word wall] simplify fraction of six-eighths (6/8), use 2, and I get three-fours (3/4)." The teacher responds, "Yes, I see you simplified the fraction six-eighths by using the common divisor of 2, and found that the equivalent fraction is three-fourths." Notice that the teacher models correct verb usage and emphasizes the key academic words that have been taught. The teacher might also refer to a previous example in which key academic words were used, or emphasize a target word by pausing momentarily or writing or pointing to it on the wall.

During interactions that have a low cognitive demand, when the concept is simple or the answer is easy, the teacher can respond to incorrect grammar. Corrective feedback in such instances can be implicit by rephrasing a student's comment in a grammatically correct way. For example, the teacher asks students if they have read about a mathematics topic in the newspaper lately. An English learner says, "Yesterday I see news about stock market and it talk about decimal numbers." The teacher's first move is to acknowledge a correct answer, and then to provide corrective feedback. "Okay," the teacher says, indicating that the student is on target. The teacher then immediately continues, "Yesterday you saw news about the stock market and there were numbers with decimals." The student replies, "Yes, I saw numbers with decimals."

As English learners often do, the student here recognizes and acknowledges the corrective feedback by using the corrected word or phrase. Feedback like this, whether in the form of mathematical rephrasing or corrective feedback, is a natural and unthreatening aspect of learning in classrooms where a safe climate has been established. Students understand that the teacher will not embarrass them and their classmates will not ridicule them.

Figure 4.4 describes several simple routines for encouraging student participation in whole-class or small-group discussions that can ease the anxiety English learners may feel about sharing their ideas. When students are working in small groups, the Think-Pair-Share strategy provides an opportunity for partner sharing prior to class sharing. Another routine to support group work is Heads Together, which facilitates small-group discussion. For whole-class discussions, a Ball-Toss routine can get even reluctant high school students to speak. Luck-of-the-Draw is another option for reducing students' resistance to speaking. Teachers will need to decide which of these strategies will most support their English learners in specific situations. When selecting a strategy to employ, it will be important for teachers to consider maintaining a safe learning environment for all students.

English learners, particularly those whose English language skills fall below the *intermediate* proficiency level, may be unsure about the meaning and use of transition words (see Figure 4.3). They may also lack the general language skills needed to discuss ideas, such as asking a clarifying question, or agreeing or disagreeing with someone's idea. Figure 4.5 presents sets of discussion sentence starters that can be enlarged and placed on laminated placards to post on the wall or hang from the ceiling. These sentence starters can help English learners to begin expressing their ideas, using common words or phrases not yet in their repertoire.

Finally, the mathematics teacher should expect English learners as well as native English speakers to vary the formality of their use of academic language depending on the context. Written academic language is typically the most formal. Formal oral presentations would also be held to the highest standards for language use. However, most spoken academic language is not formal. It falls between the formality of written academic language and the informality of social language. Even university lectures and learned discussions tend to be fragmented, containing insertions, repetitions, and deletions.[13] Similarly, the academic speech of English learners will be informal and should not be corrected for every misstep. By being strategic about when to address errors, the teacher increases the effectiveness of the feedback that is offered.

Writing prompts for specific mathematics problems can be a "writing-to-learn" activity that gives students practice in communicating their knowledge of mathematics, helps students clarify concepts, and assists teachers with informal assessment of students' understanding of mathematical language and concepts."[14] English learners at the beginning levels need scaffolding to express their

Think-Pair-Share. In Think-Pair-Share, students take a minute to think, then share answers with a partner before participating in a whole-class discussion. This allows English learners to say their ideas comfortably with a partner before sharing with the class. Think-Pair-Share is another way to build in redundancy, allowing English learners to hear an important concept described in slightly different ways, first in pairs and then in a whole-class discussion. It also provides an opportunity for modeling effective use of language.

Heads Together. Heads Together is similar to a huddle in football. The classroom is arranged in small groups, with each group seated around a worktable or with their chairs pulled into a circle. The teacher poses a question or mathematics task with a brief time limit. In each group, students stand and lean their heads close together to quietly discuss and reach agreement. When everyone in a group sits back down, the teacher knows the group is finished. Heads Together minimizes classroom noise, helps to engage all students, and signals the start and finish of small-group discussions.

Toss-the-Ball. Toss-the-Ball gets all students to participate during whole-class discussions. The teacher tosses a ball to a student who then responds (some teachers allow the first student to say "pass"). After answering, the student tosses the ball to a classmate. This student may use sentence starters to agree, disagree, build on the first student's response, or offer a different idea (see Figure 4.5 for examples). The ball can continue traveling around the room for as long as seems productive. A variation is to have different questions or vocabulary words written on tape secured to different areas of the ball. The student who catches the ball answers the topmost question.

Luck-of-the-Draw. Systems to randomize turns can relieve students of the need to volunteer to speak, making it possible for shy or reluctant students to "succumb" to the dictates of fortune. For example, in class discussions, the teacher might have all students' names written on slips of paper or tongue depressors and collected in a cup. The last student to answer draws the name of the next person to respond. Likewise, in small groups, speaking turns might depend on rolling dice or picking a card. It is often the case that students appreciate the chance to speak — they just don't want to volunteer.

ideas in writing, such as sentence frames in which they fill in parts that target key ideas. It can help English learners to start by drawing pictures or completing a graphic organizer before they tackle the writing task.

TEACHING VOCABULARY

Many mathematics textbooks and other instructional resources highlight key vocabulary words that are critical for understanding the topic[15] and that many students typically will not know. In addition, English learners may not know many other words in the text that will be crucial for their full understanding of the topic. Teachers who have observed and noted the language proficiency and backgrounds of their students will be able to strategically select and teach the key words that all their students, including their English learners, need to know.

To support English learners, the mathematics teacher will be very deliberate about what vocabulary to teach, and when to teach it. Supporting the development of students' mathematics vocabulary should be done within the context of learning concepts, not in isolation. The teacher plans activities that target key vocabulary development at key points in various phases in the lesson.[16]

FIGURE 4.5. Discussion Sentence Starters

Predicting

» I guess/predict/imagine that...

» Based on..., I infer that...

» I hypothesize that...

Asking for Clarification

» What do you mean?

» Will you explain that again?

» How did you find your answer?

Soliciting a Response

» What do you think?

» We haven't heard from you yet.

» Do you agree?

» What is your solution? How did you get it?

Affirming

» That's an interesting idea.

» I hadn't thought of that.

» I see what you mean.

Reporting a Partner's Idea

» ___ shared with me that...

» ___ pointed out to me that...

» ___ emphasized that...

» ___ concluded that...

Disagreeing

» I don't agree with you because...

» I got a different answer than you.

» I see it another way. I think...

Expressing an Opinion

» I think/believe that...

» In my opinion...

» It seems to me that...

» Based on my experience, I think...

Paraphrasing

» So you are saying that...

» In other words, you think...

» What I hear you saying is...

Acknowledging Ideas

» My idea is similar to/related to ___'s idea.

» I agree with ___ that...

» My idea builds upon ___'s idea.

Holding the Floor

» As I was saying...

» If I could finish my thought...

» What I was trying to say was...

Reporting a Group's Idea

» We decided/agreed that...

» We concluded that...

» Our group sees it differently.

» We had a different approach.

Offering a Suggestion

» Maybe we could...

» What if we...

» Here's something we might try.

Source: Adapted from *Language Strategies for Active Classroom Participation* (June 2007) with permission from Kate Kinsella. The document can be accessed as LanguageClassDiscussion.doc at http://www.sccoe.org/depts/ell/kinsella.asp. This webpage also lists many other "open access" documents that Kate Kinsella presents in her workshops.

The mathematics teacher can plan to introduce new words at the appropriate point in the lesson and repeatedly apply these new words when students speak, read, and write. For example, new vocabulary can be introduced and applied in the *introduce* stage, while connecting to prior knowledge (students' experiences or previous lessons), or in the *investigate* phase, during the exploration of a task.

Six Steps for Teaching Vocabulary

As noted, not all new vocabulary is taught at the same time. Following are six steps for teaching key vocabulary words that a teacher can use when planning a mathematics lesson. The teacher chooses the key words in the textbook that students, particularly English learners, are unlikely to know; identifies which words are most important; targets when to teach the words (during which of the three phases of instruction); and ensures ample time to teach these words. Most key words will be mathematics terms; some words may be transition words (e.g., and, but, if…then); some may be adjectives or adverbs that enrich the meaning of a mathematics term.

> **Teaching Vocabulary**
>
> » Step 1. Identify words all students need to know
>
> » Step 2. Identify words English learners need to know
>
> » Step 3. Select the highest-priority words
>
> » Step 4. Choose key words for a day's lesson
>
> » Step 5. Build from informal to formal understanding
>
> » Step 6. Plan many opportunities to apply key words

STEP 1. IDENTIFY WORDS ALL STUDENTS NEED TO KNOW

Determine which of the key words for a day's lesson is best introduced, taught, and/or reinforced at each of three phases (the words may be those highlighted in the text, those found in problem-solving contexts, or those identified by the teacher):[17]

> » **Introduce phase.** At this stage, the teacher elicits and discusses common definitions and examples from students' prior knowledge. For example, reference to "planes" during the introduce phase may only elicit students' basic knowledge of a flat surface, or perhaps even a tool to smooth a piece of wood; during the investigate phase, the mathematical definition would be added. Recognizing students' prior knowledge can guide the teacher's work as the lesson develops.

> » **Investigate phase.** During this phase, the teacher revisits the words for which students didn't understand mathematics-specific meanings and helps students refine their understanding, using formal mathematical definitions. This is also the phase at which teachers help students learn the meanings of words that will support their attempts to solve a mathematics task, either before they start exploring on their own, or as they attempt to express their reasoning in speech or writing.

> » **Summarize phase.** Toward the end of each lesson, the teacher checks for student understanding of the vocabulary and related concepts. This is the phase that allows teachers to reinforce correct definitions and to make notes on important words and concepts that should be revisited later.

STEP 2. IDENTIFY WORDS ENGLISH LEARNERS NEED TO KNOW

The mathematics teacher searches for other words in the lesson with which English speakers are already familiar, but which might be new to English learners. English learners must be able to comprehend these key words when reading the textbook, interpreting a problem-solving situation, listening to teacher talk, and engaging in class discussions. The words may include the following:

> » Mathematical terms, such as "simplify," "value," and "evaluate"

» Words that native English speakers likely know but English learners may not, such as "least" and "common"

» Transition words or phrases, such as "One solution is … *because* ..."

STEP 3. SELECT THE HIGHEST-PRIORITY WORDS

The teacher highlights the highest-priority words — those which

» are absolutely essential to understanding the lesson;

» should not be replaced with more common words because they are key academic terms in the content standards (e.g., "parabola" should not be replaced with "curved line"); and

» are key words, or what Susana Dutro and Carol Moran[18] call the "brick and mortar" words. "Bricks" are the mathematics concepts, and "mortar" is the general vocabulary that supports or connects the concepts. (For example, in the statement "If x equals 3, then y must be 15," the words "equals," "x," "y," "3," and "15" are bricks; and "if," "then," and "must be" are mortar.)

Teachers will, of course, support students in understanding additional unfamiliar yet important words that crop up during a lesson. However, teaching unfamiliar words is most effective when the teacher has anticipated the lesson's language needs and included important words in the lesson plan.

Since several words may not be addressed in the lesson plan, the teacher plans comfortable, risk-free ways during the lesson for students to flag words they do not know. For example, students might use any of the following strategies:

» Circle unfamiliar words in textbooks and/or handouts.

» Use sticky notes to identify unfamiliar words in the textbook.

» Write unfamiliar words in a section of a note-taking template that the teacher monitors, helping particular students or groups with quick definitions (when there is time, students can use dictionaries and glossaries for unfamiliar words).

» Use dialogue journals to let the teacher know what concepts and words they do not understand.

STEP 4. CHOOSE KEY WORDS FOR A DAY'S LESSON

The teacher needs to be realistic about how much new vocabulary students will be able to comprehend during one day's lesson. When the number of new words is overwhelming, the teacher can shelter the language load by using resource materials with more controlled language and illustrations, or by scanning text and substituting synonyms that students already know.

Typically, teaching no more than 10 words a day is desirable, but a teacher may choose to exceed this number when some of the words are related as synonyms/antonyms to each other or are part of a word family. Also, English learners who know a concept in their native language and only need the translated English word(s) may be able to handle more new words. Some of these known words may be *cognates*[19] — words that have the same meaning and the same or similar spellings because they derive from the same ancestor language — or words one language has borrowed from the other.

The teacher's judgment about how many words to introduce is based on knowing the students and what words they know or likely know, how difficult the new words are, and the need to maintain the focus of instruction on mathematics content. It may be that some words that don't make the cut are related to higher-priority words and can be linked to them (e.g., "ratio" is related to "fraction"). Other, lower-priority words might be defined in context, or simply replaced with known words, to make a sentence comprehensible and allow understanding of the concept to build.

STEP 5. BUILD FROM INFORMAL TO FORMAL UNDERSTANDING

The mathematics teacher needs to consider whether to introduce new words before, while, or after covering a mathematics concept, keeping in mind that learning new words naturally progresses from informal to formal understanding.[20] Typically, new words are introduced, in context, during the lesson. Informally, the teacher starts with students' own definitions, explanations, examples, or drawings for a new concept. The new word can then be formally associated with the concept.

Activating students' prior experiences or knowledge cues the teacher into ways to help guide students' learning. Their responses may be incomplete or very general at first; the teacher can gradually instruct them in a word's multiple meanings or more specific meanings. The teacher also shows students how to use context clues to determine the meaning of a word. Students keep glossaries and look up definitions in dictionaries later, in the more formal process of building understanding.[21]

Here is an example of how learning a new word can move from the informal to formal. The word "parallelogram" might be introduced informally using examples that build on students' prior knowledge, such as "a rectangle is a kind of parallelogram." Later in the lesson on polygons, this example is replaced with a formal definition, such as "A parallelogram is a quadrilateral whose opposite sides are parallel and congruent (or equal in length)." The formal definition can then be linked back to the informal by reminding students that a rectangle is a special kind of parallelogram.

STEP 6. PLAN MANY OPPORTUNITIES TO APPLY KEY WORDS

Students need many opportunities in class discussions and when working with print or written passages to hear, repeat, and apply key terms, in order to deepen and sustain their understanding of them. The mathematics teacher consciously reuses the key words, emphasizing them during teacher talk by pausing and perhaps saying the word slightly louder or pointing to the word on a wall chart.[22]

In addition to word charts and word walls, students should have key terms readily available in notebooks or personal glossaries in which they continually enter new words, brief definitions, and other cognitive supports such as illustrations or diagrams. The personal glossary primarily serves each student as a ready reference, but the teacher can draw quick reviews from student glossaries and solicit white-board answers, for example, of words, definitions, or meaningful sentences, based on recent entries.

Tools for Understanding Vocabulary and Concepts

Teachers have many options for teaching vocabulary and helping students organize and understand concepts. Teachers will find the strategies or tools found on the following pages particularly useful. However, while these tools have widely accepted applications for helping students learn words and definitions, they often connote a linear connection among concepts and, therefore, may not adequately illustrate the interrelated mathematics concepts represented by the words. Teachers need to carefully consider their mathematical goals for students when they select tools to support academic vocabulary development. For example, a Word Wall including definitions and illustrations for various types of quadrilaterals may be used throughout a unit to support students in identifying different quadrilaterals. However, during a lesson with the specific goal of helping students compare and contrast characteristics of different quadrilaterals, the teacher might have students use a Features Matrix (see page 60) to identify the characteristics of each type of quadrilateral. The tools presented in this chapter may be particularly useful for such content as logical arguments, data collection and organization, or number patterns. They will not be helpful for all words or concepts in mathematics. (See chapter 5 for tools that are helpful for representing more complex relationships and for scaffolding mathematical concepts.)

It is likely that the teacher would combine several of these tools to support students in a given lesson. Regardless of the lesson, the combination of tools would almost surely include Word Walls or Glossaries (see page 55). The Concept Organizer (see page 58) is another key tool, best used daily for perhaps two or three crucial words. Sentence Frames and Vocabulary Self-ratings (see pages 56 and 57) can be useful as pre- and post-assessments. The Features Matrix (see page 60) is useful both during a lesson and for review. List-Group-Label (see page 59) is another way for students to review, allowing them to consolidate conceptual as well as vocabulary knowledge.

We recommend that mathematics teachers use these tools to support hands-on problem solving, direct instruction, small-group work, and whole-group discussion. To determine which vocabulary building tools to provide students in a particular lesson, a teacher can try out a couple of them while planning the lesson and evaluate how well each works for clarifying particular mathematics instruction.

WORD WALL AND GLOSSARY

Purpose Word walls and glossaries help English learners develop and use academic language. Students have important vocabulary words with brief definitions readily available to use when they talk and write about their ideas.

Description *Word walls or word charts* list important academic words and phrases along with defining statements (e.g., pictures, informal definition, or example sentence). Words are entered into the word wall as they are introduced and may later be organized by topic. These lists are posted around the classroom so that students can easily see and use them. The word wall is co-constructed by the teacher and the students to create a public base of knowledge that supports the use of appropriate academic language by all students.

Glossaries are personal collections of important words defined by students and may also include illustrations or other representations. Students may also translate the words into their native languages. In addition to glossary words that students choose for themselves, the teacher may request that all students make specific entries.

Use Word Walls and Word Charts are not just for primary grades — high school students will use more academic vocabulary in their speaking and writing when they have a rich bank of words easily available.[23]

The teacher or a student adds words to wall charts as new words are introduced. In addition to key mathematics terms, the Word Wall may include other words — transition words and modifiers — that are important for English learners. Students can refer to the charts and apply the words in speaking and writing.

Words might be organized alphabetically or by word families, within topic areas. Word lists can be maintained on a computer for updating and for alternative organizations. Alternatively, large file cards can be tacked to a corkboard with the words on one side and definitions and illustrations on the other side. This allows for categorizing ideas so students see the connection between concepts, and can also be used for quick review or assessment.

There is a range of uses for a wall chart, from simply listing the words on chart paper with a brief visual cue (e.g., sketches or examples) to having a pre-formatted wall chart to identify word use and add definitions (mirroring what students have in their notebooks). Word Walls can be visible as the teacher is introducing concepts or students are engaging in problem solving; in this way, it becomes an ongoing tool to model spelling, correct usage, definitions, etc. The complexity of the format depends on the grade level and the emphasis needed for development of content knowledge understanding.

Parallel to the word wall for the class, students might build personal glossaries in their notebooks as a quick reference — especially for writing tasks — including cognates and synonyms in their native languages.

Examples Word Walls and personal glossaries take various forms depending on their particular purpose. Here is just one example. Teachers will find many additional ways to organize and utilize these tools.

Lists of related words are categorized and their meanings clarified with examples or illustrations:

Measures of Central Tendency: Finding the "Average" of a Set of Data		
Measure of central tendency (part of speech)	How to find the measure	Example using one data set *Values: 5, 2, 8, 2, 3* *Number of Values: 5*
Mean (n.)	(Sum of values) ÷ (number of values)	$(5 + 2 + 8 + 2 + 3) \div 5 = 4$ Mean is 4
Median (n.)	Arrange the data in numerical order, and find the middle value in the list.	2, 2, 3, 5, 8 ➜ median is 3
Mode (n.)	Find the value that occurs the most often.	2 occurs the most ➜ mode is 2

SENTENCE FRAMES

Purpose	English learners have a "starting place" for saying and writing their ideas, as well as models of correct grammar usage and paragraph construction.
Description	Students are prompted to create sentences based on frames that provide some sentence parts and leave blanks for others. In some cases, pictures scaffold students' understanding and ability to complete the blank portions of the sentences. Sentence Starters are types of Sentence Frames in which only the start of the sentence is given.
Use	Frames help English learners produce a complete sentence or paragraph to communicate knowledge. In addition, Sentence Frames can be used to model English grammar, while paragraph frames can be used to model writing skills. Most of a sentence is provided for English learners at early stages (*beginning, early intermediate*), and Sentence Starters are provided for more advanced English learners (*intermediate, early advanced*). Sample Sentence Frames are displayed on the wall for quick reference.
Examples	» **Sentence Starters:** A bank of sentence starters is posted in the classroom (e.g., "I agree with _____" or "I don't understand why _____"). The teacher directs students to relevant frames and encourages students to use them during a discussion or writing activity.[24] (See Figure 4.5 for more examples of Sentence Starters.)
	» **Sentence Frames:** After a lesson about geometric shapes, for example, the teacher provides students with visuals of random shapes and a list of the shapes that have been discussed. Students are asked to identify the shapes they know and explain why they believe the shape is the one they have identified, giving the appropriate characteristics. For example, students are shown a square. *Beginning* and *early intermediate* English learners are given a form with the following Sentence Frames: "The sides of this shape are … . The angles of this shape are … . This shape is called a…." English learners at the *intermediate* level may be given Sentence Frames with fewer scaffolds, for example, "This shape is called a _____ because it has … ."

VOCABULARY SELF-RATING

Purpose	This activity alerts students to the key words they will learn and helps them plan and monitor their learning. It helps students be aware of what they know, and take responsibility for what they need to learn. The teacher adjusts lessons based on a quick review of students' personal rating sheets.
Description	Students rate their knowledge of key vocabulary words before and after the *investigate* phase of the lesson. A student's self-rating is personal; it may be shared with the teacher, but it is not graded. Students rate whether they know the word (K), do not know the word (DK), or are not sure (?) at three different points: before the lesson begins, after specific vocabulary instruction, and after instruction on mathematics content (at the end of the entire lesson).
Use	» *Introduce* phase: The teacher pronounces each word and students rate their knowledge level. This alerts students to words they need to learn. A quick survey of completed columns alerts the teacher to which words to emphasize.
	» *Investigate* phase: Students rate the words again after vocabulary instruction. Students see their growth and the teacher sees which words need more attention during the content lesson.
	» *Summarize* phase: Students rate the words once again and see their growth, while the teacher sees which concepts need further discussion and what content related to the words may not be sufficiently understood.
Example	Students rate their knowledge of key words that are important in the day's lesson on division of whole numbers.

Vocabulary Self-rating

Name:			
Lesson Topic:			Period:
K: I am sure I know it	**DK**: I am sure I don't know it		**?**: I'm not sure
Word (part of speech)	Before Lesson	After Vocabulary Discussion	After Lesson
Divisor (n.)			
Division (n.)			
Quotient (n.)			
Divided (v.)			

CONCEPT ORGANIZER

Purpose   This tool provides English learners one structure for investigating in depth the meanings of selected academic vocabulary.

Description   One concept organizer is used for each new word. This tool organizes a variety of ways to understand a word's meaning: sentences, synonyms, definitions, characteristics, examples, and non-examples. If present, a prefix is noted as a clue to a word's meaning. Characteristics are phrases that may give slightly different aspects of the word's meaning. The definition broadly covers the characteristics.

Use   The teacher gives the word in context, perhaps in a sentence from the mathematics activity. The class brainstorms synonyms, definitions, characteristics, examples, and non-examples. To complete the Concept Organizer each student writes his or her own sentence that uses the word. Use the following sequence of steps to teach each new word:

» Point to the word on the word list and pronounce it; ask students to repeat the word.

» With class participation, define and describe the word, using at least a synonym or definition, and a sentence or brief explanation. Following are some options:

   – Identify one or several synonyms, or related mathematics ideas that students already know.

   – List facts/characteristics, perhaps words combined with pictures.

   – List examples and non-examples, using words, sketches, and diagrams.

   – Create a student-friendly definition or adapted definition from the textbook or a dictionary, or brainstorm a definition with students; write it on the board or a transparency while students write it on their organizers.

   – Create a sentence that implicitly defines and applies the word, or create a brief explanation (a phrase up to a few sentences).

» Students' Concept Organizers can be written on 5×7 index cards, hole-punched in the top left corner, and organized on a large key ring.

Example   Concept Organizers take various forms depending on their particular purpose. Here, the Frayer Model is used to organize information related to the concept of inequality.

Definition	**Facts/Characteristics**
An inequality is a mathematical statement that describes the relationship between two unequal quantities using the symbols $<$, $>$, $\leq$, or $\geq$.	Relates two unequal expressions. The value of one expression is greater than or less than the other.
Examples	**Non-examples**
20 oz. $<$ 25 oz. π is greater than 3 $2 \geq x$	5 is equal to 4 + 1 $a = 197$ $3x$

*(Center label: **Inequality**)*

LIST-GROUP-LABEL

Purpose Groups of vocabulary words are taught as word families, or new words are added to existing family groups after they are taught. Organizing words into word families and concept categories promotes schema formation and conceptual understanding. For reference and review, students can quickly search the charts and recognize relationships.

Description Known words relevant to a lesson are organized by categories given by the teacher or created by student groups. The teacher guides students to see how words are associated. Word families can be classified by relationship (e.g., synonym/antonym) or conceptual characteristics (e.g., numbers, types of quadrilaterals, measures of central tendency).

Use The whole class may brainstorm an initial list of words about a topic and the teacher records them on the board or a transparency; then small groups organize them by categories and give labels to the categories. When words have multiple meanings in different disciplines, teachers of different subjects can collaborate and teach the multiple meanings explicitly, so students see both the connections and subtle differences in meanings.

Examples The teacher asks student groups to construct a chart associating types of length measurement units with their characteristics. Students then share group charts and create a class chart to build or construct common knowledge.

Numbers	
Types	Characteristics
Whole	
Rational	
Irrational	
Imaginary	

Functions	
Types	Characteristics
Linear	
Quadratic	
Exponential	
Trigonometric	

FEATURES MATRIX

Purpose Students see concept words and their relationships visually reinforced. Similar but frequently confused terms are clarified; similarities and differences within a category are graphically represented.

Description Characteristics are compared across a range of objects or topics. Cells in the matrix are marked Yes (present), No (not present), or Maybe (sometimes present).

Use Students work in pairs or small groups to complete a matrix first modeled by the teacher. The matrix may be completed as part of note taking during reading and instruction or to summarize and review afterward. Student groups may be encouraged to add characteristics in a few additional columns on the right. After completing the matrix, students use sentences orally or in writing to describe the characteristics present or not present in an object or topic. (For example, "A square has four sides of equal length and 4 right (90°) angles.")

Example This features matrix helps students distinguish among various quadrilaterals.

Type of Quadrilateral	Right angle	Parallel sides	Opposite sides equal length
Parallelogram	Maybe	Yes (2 pairs)	Yes
Rectangle	Yes	Yes (2 pairs)	Yes
Square	Yes	Yes (2 pairs)	Yes (all four sides)
Trapezoid	No	Yes (1 pair)	Maybe
Rhombus	Maybe	Yes (2 pairs)	Yes

ENDNOTES FOR CHAPTER 4

[1] Harlev, R. (2005). Contented learning. *Language, 4*(9), 22–27.

Bay-Williams, J.M., & Herrera, S. (2007). Is "just good teaching" enough to support the learning of English language learners? Insights from sociocultural learning theory. In W.G. Martin, M.E. Strutchens, & P.C. Elliott (Eds.), *The learning of mathematics: Sixty-ninth yearbook* (pp. 43–63). Reston, VA: National Council of Teachers of Mathematics.

Freeman, D.J. (2004). Teaching in the context of English-language learners: What we need to know. In M. Sadowski (Ed.), *Teaching immigrant and second-language students: Strategies for success* (pp. 7–20). Cambridge, MA: Harvard Education Press.

[2] Gibbons, P. (2002). *Scaffolding language, scaffolding learning.* Portsmouth, NH: Heinemann.

[3] Short, D. (1993). Assessing integrating language and content. *TESOL Quarterly, 27*(4), 627–656.

Bay-Williams, J.M., & Herrera, S. (2007). Is "just good teaching" enough to support the learning of English language learners? Insights from sociocultural learning theory. In W.G. Martin, M.E. Strutchens, & P.C. Elliott (Eds.), *The learning of mathematics: Sixty-ninth yearbook* (pp. 43–63). Reston, VA: National Council of Teachers of Mathematics.

[4] Clegg, J. (Ed.) (1996). *Mainstreaming ESL: Case studies in integrating ESL students into the mainstream curriculum.* Clevedon, UK. Multilingual Matters.

[5] Kang, H., & Pham, K.T. (1995, March). *From 1 to Z: Integrating math and language learning.* Paper presented at the 29th annual meeting of the Teachers of English to Speakers of Other Languages, Long Beach, CA. (ERIC Document Reproduction Service No. ED 381 031)

[6] Martin, T.S. (Ed.). (2007). *Mathematics teaching today* (2nd ed.). Reston, VA: National Council of Teachers of Mathematics.

[7] Anstrom, K. (1999). *Preparing secondary education teachers to work with English language learners: Mathematics* (NCBE Resource Collection Series, No. 14). Washington, DC: National Clearinghouse for Bilingual Education.

Cambell, A.E., Adams, V.M., & Davis, G.E. (2007). Cognitive demands and second-language learners: A framework for analyzing mathematics instructional contexts. *Mathematical Thinking and Learning, 9*(1), 3–30.

Ellerton, N.F., & Clarkson, P.C. (1996). Language factors in mathematics teaching and learning. In A.J. Bishop, K. Clements, C. Keitel, J. Kilpatrick, & C. Laborde (Eds.), *International handbook of mathematics education* (pp. 987–1033). Dordrecht: Kluwer.

Mestre, J. (1988). The role of language comprehension in mathematics and problem solving. In R. Cocking & J. Mestre (Eds.), *Linguistic and cultural influences on learning mathematics* (pp. 201–220). Hillsdale, NJ: Lawrence Erlbaum.

[8] Monroe, E.E., & Panchyshyn, R. (1995). Vocabulary considerations for teaching mathematics. *Childhood Education, 72* (2), 80–83.

Laborde, C. (1990). Language and mathematics. In P. Nesher & J. Kilpatrick (Eds.), *Mathematics and cognition: A research synthesis by the international group for the Psychology of Mathematics Education* (pp. 53–69). Cambridge: Cambridge University Press.

[9] Hayden, D., & Cuevas, G. (1990). *Pre-algebra lexicon.* Washington, DC: Center for Applied Linguistics.

[10] Anstrom, K. (1999). *Preparing secondary education teachers to work with English language learners: Mathematics* (NCBE Resource Collection Series, No. 14). Washington, DC: National Clearinghouse for Bilingual Education.

[11] Jarrett, D. (1999). *The inclusive classroom: Teaching mathematics and science to English-language learners.* Portland, OR: Northwest Regional Educational Laboratory.

[12] Mason, J., Burton, L., & Stacey, K. (1982). *Thinking mathematically.* London: Addison-Wesley.

[13] Swales, J.M. (2005). Academically speaking. *Language Magazine, 4*(8), 30–34. Conclusions based on analysis of 1.7 million transcribed words of University of Michigan speeches from lectures, office hours, meetings, dissertation defenses, and so forth, collected between 1997 and 2002.

[14] Kang, H., & Pham, K.T. (1995, March). *From 1 to Z: Integrating math and language learning.* Paper presented at the 29th annual meeting of the Teachers of English to Speakers of Other Languages, Long Beach, CA. (ERIC Document Reproduction Service No. ED 381 031)

[15] Marzano, R.J., & Pickering, D.J. (2005). *Building academic vocabulary teacher's manual*. Alexandria, VA: Association for Supervision and Curriculum Development. The authors have identified nearly 8,000 words in national standards documents in 11 subject areas for grade spans K–2, 3–5, 6–8, and 9–12. The math word list is on pages W1-8.

[16] Dornan, R., Rosen, L.M., & Wilson, M. (2005). Lesson designs for reading comprehension and vocabulary development. In P.A. Richard-Amato, & M.A. Snow, (Eds.), *Academic success for English language learners*, (pp. 248–274). White Plains, NY: Pearson Education, Inc.

[17] The two websites below for identifying (and defining) key terms are representative of the online vocabulary resources available for teachers and students:

http://www.mathwords.com for beginning algebra through calculus words.

http://www.harcourtschool.com/glossary/math2/ for grades K–6.

[18] Dutro, S., & Moran, C. (2003). Rethinking English language instruction: An architectural approach. In G.G. Garcia (Ed.), *English learners: Reaching the highest level of English literacy*. Newark, DE: International Reading Association.

[19] English and Spanish have many cognates from Latin-based words (e.g., problem/problema and dictionary/diccionario). False cognates, or falso amigos, on the other hand, can trip students up (see http://spanish.about.com/cs/vocabulary/a/obviouswrong.htm for the tricky actual/actual, discutir/discuss, ignorar/ignore, realizar/realize, and others).

[20] Marzano, R.J., & Pickering, D.J. (2005). *Building academic vocabulary teacher's manual* (p. 16). Alexandria, VA: Association for Supervision and Curriculum Development.

[21] Print dictionaries recommended by Kate Kinsella for use with English learners include the following:

Early intermediate level in grades 4–9: *The Basic Newbury House Dictionary of American English* (1998) by Heinle & Heinle.

Intermediate level in grades 6–12: *Newbury House Dictionary with Thesaurus* (2004) by Heinle & Heinle; *Longman Dictionary of American English* (1997) by Longman.

Advanced level in grades 7–12 and college: *Longman Advanced American Dictionary* (2000) by Longman.

Beginning through *advanced* levels: *Thorndike Barnhart Dictionary* (1999) by Scott Forsman.

[22] Marzano and Pickering offer a range of activities and academically oriented games for reviewing and applying word meanings. Marzano, R.J., & Pickering, D.J. (2005). *Building academic vocabulary teacher's manual*. Alexandria, VA: Association for Supervision and Curriculum Development.

[23] Gibbons, P. (2002). *Scaffolding language, scaffolding learning*. Portsmouth, NH: Heinemann

[24] For sentence starters that are appropriate for mathematics through middle school, see http://www.wested.org/cs/we/view/rs/781.

CHAPTER 5
Scaffolding Mathematics Learning

The elegant metaphor of "scaffolding" comes to the field of learning[1] from the rough-and-tumble world of construction sites, where temporary frameworks of platforms erected around a building allow workers to reach with their drills, hammers, and brushes areas that otherwise would be out of range. Likewise, a mathematics teacher uses scaffolding strategies to temporarily support students while they build new mathematics skills and knowledge — at a higher level than they could reach without such assistance.[2]

It is important to note that scaffolding is not just another word for helping. As Pauline Gibbons specifies, "It is a special kind of help that assists learners to move toward new skills, concepts, or levels of understanding. Scaffolding is thus a temporary assistance by which a teacher helps a learner know how to do something, so that the learner will later be able to complete a similar task alone."[3] Gibbons warns that scaffolding is not about simplifying a learning task and ultimately watering down curriculum. The importance of scaffolding is that it allows a teacher to provide authentic and challenging tasks to all students, with the supports that allow them to be individually successful.

All students benefit from teachers who guide and support them as they construct new knowledge. English learners, our focus here, require extra support if they are to master a rigorous, standards-based curriculum. Every student has the right to equal access to the curriculum. Scaffolding is a way for teachers to keep content at a high level, yet still provide access to the variety of students in the classroom.

We begin the chapter by discussing how to use scaffolding strategies, including four "big ideas" to simplify their use and an outline of a lesson plan that integrates vocabulary strategies from chapter 4 and scaffolding strategies described in this chapter. Next, we present four options for scaffolding mathematics reading materials. Last, we describe seven specific strategies that allow mathematics teachers to scaffold learning for English learners. These strategies were chosen because they apply to teaching mathematics, can be learned fairly quickly, and can be practiced in the classroom quite easily. Research has found these strategies to be effective with the general student population[4] and with English learners.[5]

We assume that many mathematics teachers are familiar with at least some of these strategies. What may be new is how they can be integrated, possibly increasing their effectiveness for English learners. For example, an enhanced word wall integrates illustrations and brief definitions as in a concept organizer. If key academic words are written on paper strips, they can be rearranged into a graphic organizer during a lesson to represent relationships between concepts. In addition, we imagine that some teachers may know how to use a strategy in a whole-class lesson but not know how to differentiate, or modify, its use to fit different levels of English learners.

If a strategy is entirely new for a teacher, it might be necessary to go to other resource materials or experienced colleagues to learn more about using it effectively. However, we purposefully selected strategies that are fairly quick and easy to learn.

HOW TO USE SCAFFOLDING STRATEGIES

The scaffolding strategies in this chapter benefit all students in the classroom and can be implemented in whole-class activities, but differentiated according to students' needs. The teacher structures the use of a strategy to give appropriate kinds of support to students at different English language development levels to ensure that all students can access rigorous content. (Chapter 7 presents classroom scenarios that integrate scaffolding and differentiated instruction.)

Because scaffolding in teaching, as in construction, is temporary, the teacher has a plan to reduce or fade the level of support provided as students become increasingly accomplished. The teacher's goal is to move learners from dependence on teacher-designated strategies to independent application of strategies for their own purposes and in a variety of settings. So, when introducing a new strategy, the teacher models its use and discusses its purpose. The teacher discusses classroom rules that underpin using the strategy, such as respecting others' opinions, valuing diversity of beliefs, and other acceptable social learning behaviors. Then the teacher guides student practice. Finally, when students have sufficiently internalized the strategy and understand its purpose, process, and various uses, they apply it independently during group and individual learning tasks.

We use the example of graphic organizers to concretely show the shift from teacher to student for the selection and use of this specific scaffolding technique. More detailed examples of graphic organizers are described on pages 70–72.

» The teacher shows a model of a graphic organizer such as a web or bubble organizer, explains its purpose, and shows how to use it with a very specific example.

» The teacher provides small groups with a graphic organizer template that is blank or partially completed to different degrees depending on a group's ELD level; groups complete the task together while the teacher monitors and checks for understanding; then they debrief.

» Students work in groups to apply the graphic organizer in a few lessons and then work independently to apply it. When working independently, some students will be given almost complete, some partially complete, and some blank organizers according to their need for scaffolded support.

» As students collect a bank of graphic organizers (e.g., webs, Venn diagrams, T-charts, cycles), the teacher guides students to compare and contrast their applications in different contexts or for different tasks, so students learn how to select the appropriate organizer for new topics or tasks.

» When the teacher systematically and frequently has students use the organizers, students build fluency and self-reliance.

Figure 5.1 describes four "big ideas" that teachers should keep in mind as they group students and select strategies to differentiate instruction according to students' needs.

FIGURE 5.1. **Big Ideas That Simplify Differentiating Instruction**

Big Idea 1: **Group Students to Provide Access for All Proficiency Levels**	To avoid a one-size-fits-all approach, a teacher considers which strategies need to be tailored to fit different levels of English learners, and when to group English learners to interact with students at the same language level (homogenous groups) or students who are more proficient in English (heterogeneous group).
	Many teachers do not have students at all five English learner levels in their classrooms (see chapter 3 for details about the five levels). For those who do, one approach is to combine students at contiguous proficiency levels into three groups. First, form an English fluent group by combining *early advanced* and *advanced* English learners, along with native English-speaking students, who can all benefit from the same types of scaffolding strategies. Second, form an English intermediate group by combining *early intermediate* students who are ready for more challenge with *intermediate* English learners. Third, form an English novice group by combining *early intermediate* English learners who still need extensive linguistic support with *beginning* learners.
	The teacher assigns students to work together in these novice, intermediate, and fluent groups during the occasional activities that benefit learners interacting in a homogenous group. Most of the time the teacher forms groups of students at different English proficiency levels so that students have multiple opportunities to practice a variety of communication skills, including rephrasing, asking for clarification, and using their native language. An advantage of heterogeneous grouping is that novice English learners experience "model" language use by more advanced English speakers. The teacher still must provide differentiation for English learners within these groups, such as note-taking templates that scaffold writing for novice, intermediate, and advanced English learners.
Big Idea 2: **Use Strategies That Work for All Students**	Some instructional strategies work well for all or most students and do not need differentiation for students at different English learner levels. English learners as well as other students whose strength is learning visually benefit when visual representations (e.g., illustrations, graphic organizers) accompany oral discussions of new concepts. English learners and other students whose strength is learning kinesthetically benefit from hands-on investigations. Teachers who know their students' backgrounds can explain difficult, abstract mathematics concepts by offering analogies that are relevant to students' lives and cultures.
Big Idea 3: **Use a Strategy Throughout the Lesson**	A specific strategy need not be limited to one time use within one phase of a mathematics activity. A strategy can be used throughout much of a lesson. For example, the teacher may begin creating a word wall and graphic organizer as simple charts during the *introduce* phase, add and expand words and concepts during the *investigate* phase, and guide the students to apply their developing vocabulary during the *summarize* phase. Routine use of a strategy throughout the year helps all students focus on learning mathematics concepts rather than on learning how to use new strategies.
Big Idea 4: **Make Connections Between Strategies**	The teacher can identify connections among strategies and make those connections explicit for students. For example, a concept organizer is used only for the most important words on a word wall, providing more depth of understanding. Furthermore, one strategy can be embedded in another. For example, sentence frames and visuals such as diagrams and brief graphic organizers can be embedded in Cornell-style notes.[6]

Source: Adapted from collaborative work between WestEd and Secondary Science Education in Los Angeles Unified School District, May 2007.

HOW TO SCAFFOLD READING MATERIALS

English learners below the *early advanced* level, as well as other students struggling with literacy skills, may have difficulty independently reading a mathematics textbook or other written text (e.g., complex activity sheets). To ensure that English learners can fully comprehend the content in mathematics texts, teachers need to integrate strategies for scaffolding mathematics activities into their lesson preparation and delivery. In general, we recommend that students do not read long text passages until they are well into the *investigative* or *summary* phase of a lesson, and the teacher has explained key unknown words, terms, and phrases, or substituted familiar words in their place. (Chapter 7 illustrates lessons that utilize the reading scaffolds described below.)

Each of the options below will be most powerful when used in conjunction with central strategies for inquiry-based mathematics.

> » Provide engaging, concrete activities to front-load key content and functional vocabulary in context, building conceptual understanding during the *introduce* and *investigate* phases. Enter key words on a Word Wall, Concept Organizer, or graphic organizer. Students can then reference these key words throughout the lesson.

> » Annotate brief definitions of key words in the margin of the page.

> » When designing activity sheets, keep sentences short and contextualized with illustrations whenever possible. You might create two alternative activity sheets, one with text structures at grade level, and another with text structures comprehensible for English learners below the *early advanced* level.

> » Provide students with meaningful questions to answer, and use Think Alouds and model reading strategies such as reciprocal teaching and assisted note taking, so that students will be able to apply metacognitive reading skills to make sense of the text and record information in notebooks.

> » Pair English learners with more literacy-proficient students to collaboratively read textbook excerpts as part of the *summarize* phase. Monitor groups to ensure all students are challenged and meaningfully engaged. Rotate among individuals or small groups, asking probing and clarifying questions.

SEVEN STRATEGIES FOR SCAFFOLDING MATHEMATICS LEARNING

Listed below are descriptions of each of seven strategies to scaffold learning for English learners. Strategies 1–4 are primarily used in activities such as direct instruction and teacher-led student conversations, while strategies 5–7 are student activities:

1. **Visuals.** These include nonlinguistic representations (e.g., photos, models, real objects, and graphic organizers that visually represent the relationships among ideas. (See page 70.)

2. **Cues.** Cueing strategies include three types. *Hints* directly frame or preview the learning. *Questions* reinforce what has been taught and check for understanding. *Advance organizers* orient students to upcoming important content. (See page 73.)

3. **Think Aloud.** The teacher uses Think Aloud to verbalize his or her own thought processes while solving a mathematics item, explaining a solution, or discussing ideas within a small-group setting. (See page 75.)

4. **KWL+.** The teacher starts a lesson by recording students' responses to questions about what they already know (K) and what they want to know (W). At the end of a lesson the teacher records what has been learned (L). The "+" aspect of KWL+ refers to the final step of making connections among the three categories of information. (See page 76.)

Strategies 5–7 are primarily student activities; the teacher guides students while they practice individual and team learning:

5. **Think-Pair-Share.** In Think-Pair-Share, the teacher poses a challenging, open-ended question and gives students one or two minutes to think; student pairs discuss their ideas, and then pairs share ideas with a larger group or the whole class. (See page 77.)

6. **Summarizing.** In Summarizing, students must comprehend and distill information into a parsimonious, synthesized form — in their own words. (See page 78.)

7. **Reciprocal Teaching.** As a reading activity of text or of word problems, in small groups, students follow a structured dialogue that involves four processes that good readers use — questioning, summarizing, clarifying, and predicting. (See page 79.)

A sample outline for a differentiated high school lesson plan on triangle congruency is displayed as Figures 5.2 and 5.3 on pages 68 and 69. Each figure is part of a single lesson plan. Figure 5.2 shows scaffolding strategies the teacher will use during each of the three phases of the lesson — introduce, investigate, and summarize. These strategies include ways to teach vocabulary and scaffold content learning, and are appropriate for a wide diversity of students in the mainstream classroom. Figure 5.3 shows how certain strategies are adapted for students at various levels of English language development. A blank row indicates that no special adaptation is needed (i.e., it's suitable for all levels of English language proficiency).

In the pages that follow, we describe each strategy, including some examples of how it may be combined with or embedded in other strategies. We encourage all teachers to look for ways to integrate these strategies into their mathematics lessons. Each strategy can be used in many, if not all, of the three mathematics phases; for instance, a graphic organizer (see "Visuals," pages 70–72) can be reused in the same form or with increasing elaboration as students review and build upon concepts and connections they have learned and discovered.

FIGURE 5.2. Conceptual Flow of Learning Activities Within the Three Instructional Phases

Overarching Question: How do you identify congruent triangles?

		Introduce	Investigate	Summarize
		Visual representation of congruent triangles	Sort triangles by congruency. Discuss sorting methods. Define and give examples and non-examples of congruent triangles.	Theorems regarding congruent triangles. Application in other mathematical situations
		Assess: Hand gestures regarding agreement and understanding of congruent triangles and sorting methods; white boards or student notes showing sorting methods and examples or non-examples of congruent triangles; quiz about identifying congruent triangles (English learners complete sentence frames)		
Scaffolding Strategies	**Enhanced Word Wall**	Informally define words from KWL chart and directions for task.	Add words and informal definitions or illustrations from discussions.	Use vocabulary in discussion and writing.
	Concept Organizer	Begin to describe characteristics, examples, and non-examples of key phrases.	Add descriptions or illustrations to concept organizer. Reference tool	Reference tool
	Sentence Frames		Modeled language for task notes. Assessment – quiz	
	Graphic Organizer Visuals/Realia	Illustrations of triangles	Sketches of congruent triangles	
	Think Aloud	Show shapes and talk about characteristics.	Demonstrate comparing two triangles.	Apply conclusions to another shape.
	KWL Chart ("Know," "Want to Know," "Learned")	K–W with visuals: Elicit from students.	W–L: Elicit from students and help students explain.	L: Elicit from students.
	Think-Pair-Share	Discuss key vocabulary and shapes.	Discuss vocabulary and comparisons of triangles.	Compare other shapes.
	Reading and Media Materials	View example shapes and descriptions in written text.	Read activity directions and supplemental information.	Read theorems and formal definition of "congruent."

Source: Adapted from Carr, J., Sexton, U., & Lagunoff, R. (2007). *Making Science Accessible to English Learners: A Guidebook for Teachers*. San Francisco, CA: WestEd.

FIGURE 5.3. **Scaffolding Strategies Modified by Academic Language Skill Levels**

		Beginning/ Advanced Beginning	Intermediate	Early Fluent/Fluent
		Heterogeneous grouping for all activities except reading texts		
Scaffolding Strategies	**Enhanced Word Wall**			
	Concept Organizer			
	Sentence Frames	Identify key concepts.	Describe key concepts.	Explain, infer, generalize.
	Graphic Organizer	Identify key ideas.	Provide some supporting details.	Provide all critical details.
	Think Aloud			
	KWL Chart ("Know," "Want to Know," "Learned")			
	Think-Pair-Share			
	Reading and Media Materials	Leveled text with support; notes with sentence frames	Leveled text; group read and take notes	Textbook group read and take notes
			Groups share information; revise notes.	

Source: Adapted from Carr, J., Sexton, U., & Lagunoff, R. (2007). *Making Science Accessible to English Learners: A Guidebook for Teachers*. San Francisco, CA: WestEd.

VISUALS, INCLUDING GRAPHIC ORGANIZERS

Purpose By generating visual illustrations to go along with information, as well as by creating graphic representations for that information, students are putting the information to work, necessarily constructing meaning as they do so. Usually, the primary method of presenting new knowledge to students is in linguistic form — by using words. When teachers help students create nonlinguistic representations of new learning, as with illustrations or symbols or by organizing information graphically, it increases students' opportunities to learn. The more that learners use both systems of representation, linguistic and nonlinguistic, the better they are able to think about and recall knowledge.

Description Visuals can be real objects, models, demonstrations, pictures, illustrations, or videos and other visual media (e.g., webcasts, animations).

Graphic organizers are visual tools for recording and recalling important information. Organizers may have labels (words, phrases), illustrations, and use spatial orientation with lines or arrows to show organization and connections. Common graphic organizers include the following: KWL chart, flowchart, cause-and-effect map, matrix, classification map, spider (web) map, Venn diagram, T-chart, fishbone chart, and sequence of events.

Use Graphic organizers can be used for ELD or content area instruction and assessment. They can be used in conjunction with lecture and discussion; they can be embedded in the use of KWL charts and note taking. They can be useful learning and assessment tools, especially for *early intermediate* to *intermediate* English learners who are not yet adept at using complex grammar and function words to connect ideas in English. During learning, graphic organizers combine visual representation with oral discussion, helping English learners connect concepts. During assessment, graphic organizers help English learners show and communicate what they understand, as an alternative to or in support of a long, complex oral or written response (e.g., many connected sentences). A graphic organizer can help all students organize their thoughts before writing an essay or research report.

Examples A variety of websites and other resources feature graphic organizers, tools for generating graphic organizers, and student samples across a range of content areas. The examples offered below have valuable mathematics applications.

DESCRIBING

Bubble Map

This simple format can be used to collect ideas or attributes, especially in a group or individual brainstorm. The teacher or students can suggest how to show the relationships among ideas. Here, the structure supports students in recognizing the general attributes of parallelograms and the particular attributes of specific types of parallelograms.

VISUALS, INCLUDING GRAPHIC ORGANIZERS (CONTINUED)

Examples
(continued)

COMPARING AND CONTRASTING

Matrix

A matrix is especially useful for comparing a number of items across a number of distinctions or attributes.

Function	$y = x2$	$y = -x2$	$y = (-x)2$
Degree	Second	Second	Second
Graph	Parabola	Parabola	Parabola
Convex/Concave	Concave	Convex	Concave

Venn Diagram

Venn diagrams organize and compare sets of information. Enclosed shapes show ideas or characteristics that are unique and/or overlap for two or more topics.

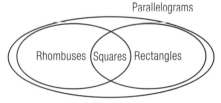

Parallelograms

Rhombuses · Squares · Rectangles

CLASSIFYING AND CATEGORIZING

Spiderweb (also called a concept map or organizer)

"Legs" from the central idea (body) often are categories such as properties or characteristics of an object; lines from each leg are the important details, facts, instances, or other type of evidence to support and describe the category.

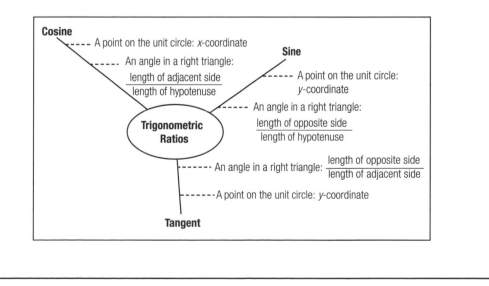

VISUALS, INCLUDING GRAPHIC ORGANIZERS (CONTINUED)

Examples
(continued)

Q&A Web

The teacher establishes major questions about an idea or object, preferably questions that have more than one answer; then students generate answers. Small groups might be assigned one question to work on together and report back to the class.

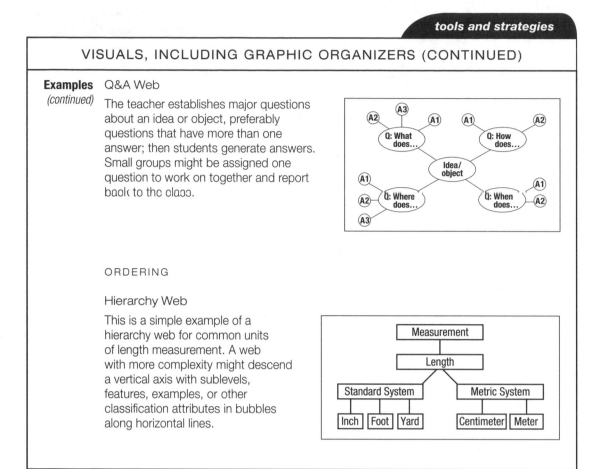

ORDERING

Hierarchy Web

This is a simple example of a hierarchy web for common units of length measurement. A web with more complexity might descend a vertical axis with sublevels, features, examples, or other classification attributes in bubbles along horizontal lines.

CUES

Purpose Cues include *hints, advance organizers,* and *questions* that are used to focus student thinking and reasoning on pertinent information and help them build bridges among related concepts or chunks of information. All three approaches engage students in thinking by activating their prior knowledge and helping them organize it.

Description The teacher provides cues as *hints* that directly frame or preview learning. Cues can be a reminder of how information was already presented, to guide students' recall and reasoning. Cues are often given to support English learners during questioning and presentation of an advance organizer. *Advance organizers* orient students to upcoming important content. They may take the form of an outline, skimming a chapter, or graphic organizers. Advance organizers bridge between what the student already knows and the material that will be taught next. Advance organizers can be embedded in the "K" or "know" part of a KWL+ chart.

The teacher uses *questions* about what has already been taught to reinforce or check understanding about important information or when modeling procedures, such as predicting and hypothesizing. These questions may be used to elicit higher-order thinking processes such as summarizing, analyzing, and making inferences. These questions should not only be about basic factual information.

Students use questions themselves to ask for clarification or indicate what they would like to learn, such as during the "W" or "what do you want to learn" part of a KWL+ chart. Students' questions can lead to class discussion that engages all students in listening to one another's thinking and offering ideas while practicing the use of academic language. Students' questions alert the teacher to what students know, do not know, or misunderstand. When a student's question reflects a misconception, it is an opportunity for further exploration, with the teacher guiding class discussion.

Use In addition to the uses described above, cues are used as a prereading activity to build background knowledge or at the start of a lesson to alert students to what will be taught and to connect to their personal and prior learning context. Cues may be used in conjunction with teaching key vocabulary words, especially for English learners.

Example As an advance organizer for a task that asks students to investigate a pattern of triangles, the teacher draws a table with three columns labeled "figure number," "number of sticks," and "addends." The teacher checks for understanding by discussing the column labels with the class. Before each figure in the pattern is drawn, the teacher provides a cue about the figure by asking a question (e.g., "How many triangles are in the figure?" or "How many sticks/lines are in the figure?").

Figure Number (N)	Number of Sticks (S)	Addends

CUES (CONTINUED)

Example
(continued) After observing the growing pattern of triangles, students record the number of triangles in each figure in a T-chart. Students are asked to state the pattern they observe and use that information to draw the fourth figure.

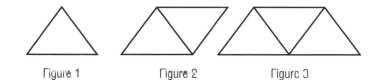

Figure 1   Figure 2   Figure 3

During the lesson, the teacher monitors pairs or small groups as they gather data and organize it into the table or graph to answer questions about the data. For groups needing assistance, the teacher asks probing and clarifying questions instead of providing easy answers. For example:

» Consider how the number of sticks changes from Figure 1 to Figure 2. How many sticks are added to create each new Figure (the recursive rule)?

» Where in the chart do you see the recursive rule?

» Draw the figure with 4 triangles. How many sticks did you add to Figure 3 to make Figure 4?

» Using your strategy for finding the pattern, find the number of sticks needed for Figure 5. Complete the table.

Figure Number (N)	Number of Sticks (S)	Addends
1	3	3 (one triangle)
2	5	3 + 2
3	7	3 + 2 + 2
4	9	3 + 2 + 2 + 2
5	11	3 + 2 + 2 + 2 + 2

» Describe in words the recursive rule, which states how the number of sticks (S) changes from figure to figure. Refer to the geometric figures in your answer.

» What is the relationship between the figure number and the number of addends shown in the table?

» How might that relationship help you find the explicit rule that allows you to find the number of sticks needed for ANY size figure?

THINK ALOUD

Purpose The teacher uses Think Alouds to make mathematical thinking transparent. Think Alouds can be used to teach comprehension skills, scaffold reading of difficult informational text, or model thought processes in an investigation or exploration. Think Alouds can be used to explicitly connect text and visual concepts and express association, time sequence, or cause and effect. Think Alouds also are used by students to verbalize their thinking as they present their solution strategies for a given task.

Description The teacher verbalizes his or her own thought processes while orally considering a situation that presents a question to answer, while modeling the steps toward answering that question, while interpreting and summarizing the solution to the question during a class discussion. The teacher orally models the interactive nature of comprehending a concept and mathematical thinking. Think Aloud may be used in conjunction with taking notes or constructing diagrams or graphic organizers. Think Aloud makes "visible" the thinking processes, decisions, connections, and clarifications of actively trying to make meaning. Think Aloud also is a way to model using the academic language of mathematics before asking students to practice it in their conversations and writing.

Use The teacher models out loud what mathematical thinking might sound like given a context. The teacher gradually fades out the modeling by stopping less often during a lesson to model thinking or by providing less prompting, while fading in opportunities for students to practice thinking aloud.

When students Think Aloud, the teacher may find that students have different perceptions or use alternative solution strategies to approach a mathematical question. When students verbalize their thoughts and rationales, the teacher can gain insights into how they think, identify misconceptions or faulty reasoning, and guide them to proper mathematical thinking.

Example The teacher may Think Aloud while orally reading a mathematics task to the students, stopping along the way to orally evaluate how the information read fits into the context; that is, whether the information is necessary to answer the question or is superfluous. Here is an example:

> While transforming the standard form for a linear equation, $Ax + By = C$, into y-intercept form, $y = mx + b$, I describe my thinking and each solution step as I model it on the board for students to see. "I want to write the equation so that it relates the value of y to the value of x. I move Ax to the other expression in the equation by subtracting Ax from both expressions: $Ax + By - Ax = C - Ax$. Doing this allows me to isolate the y term and continue on to find its value. Next, I simplify the equation: $By = C - Ax$. Now I divide both expressions by B so that $1y$ (or just y) is the expression on the left: $By/B = (C - Ax)/B$. I distribute the division by B to each term and simplify the equation: $y = C/B - (A/B)x$. Using the transitive property, I rewrite the equation so that the term including x is written before the other term: $y = (-A/B)x + C/B$. I can represent $-A/B$ with m and C/B with b so that the equation shows y-intercept form: $y = mx + b$." Follow-ups may include pointing to the problem on the white board and asking students to restate what I was thinking aloud at any point in the solution steps.

KWL+

Purpose	Eliciting from students what they know and want to know, and then what they have learned about a topic serves to get students ready to construct new knowledge, build interest in the topic, and appreciate what they are learning. Student responses help the teacher adjust the lesson to fit students' needs, preconceptions, misconceptions, and interests and to monitor their understanding.
Description	This is a reading-thinking strategy and tool. The teacher writes on a three-column chart students' responses to questions about what is already known (K) about the topic to be studied, what students want to know (W), and then what has been learned after the reading or lesson (L). In addition (+), the teacher draws lines or uses a graphic organizer to show connections among the recorded KWL information.
Use	In advance of the lesson, the teacher can check for individual understanding (K) by asking students to write or otherwise indicate their responses individually before asking for class responses. Any knowledge gaps or misunderstandings (e.g., personal or cultural beliefs not supported by math) that arise will alert the teacher to areas of the lesson needing special attention. Asking what students want to know (W) connects to their personal interests and builds motivation to learn more. Asking what students learned (L) allows them to consolidate their learning and identify gaps in knowledge they still have. Graphically mapping (+) this information helps to organize and connect ideas in the chart. The KWL+ chart can be used at all levels to review, predict, inquire, summarize, and check for understanding.
Examples	The teacher asks, "What do you know about making a bar graph?" and writes students' responses in the "K" column of the KWL chart.
	Then the teacher asks what students want to know about graphing and records their questions in the "W" column. At important points during the lesson, the teacher asks students what they just learned and enters responses in the "L" column. The teacher draws lines to connect old and new information to the inquiry questions and summarizes the connections (+ mapping). The "L" column might incorporate the results of note taking or graphic organizers. Information might be reorganized into categories or as main ideas and supporting details.
	In another example, specific to scaffolding an assignment with a task worksheet, the teacher reads aloud the information provided on the worksheet; asks students what important information has been provided; and writes appropriate responses in the "K" column of the KWL chart. Next, the teacher reads aloud the procedural instructions on the worksheet; asks students what they want to know; and enters appropriate responses in the "W" column. At the end of the activity, strategies that students used to solve the problem and their answers are entered into the "L" column.

THINK-PAIR-SHARE

Purpose Think-Pair-Share engages all students simultaneously. It gives students a chance to think about a question, share information with a partner, and consider a peer's point of view in a low-risk situation. This can be especially valuable for English learners and structures a way for them to rehearse for whole-class participation. Students are typically more willing to respond in a whole-class conversation after they have had a chance to discuss their ideas with a classmate.

Description The teacher poses a challenging, open-ended question and gives students a minute or two to think about it and start to formulate an answer. Then, in pairs, students discuss their ideas for a few minutes. To protect the opportunity of partners to have equal speaking time, the teacher may want to set time limits and have partners trade speaking and listening roles at a given signal. After the partner discussions, the teacher invites partnership reports, randomly calls on students, or takes a classroom vote.

Use This strategy can be used to apply academic vocabulary, review and summarize what was taught or read, brainstorm ideas, or explore opinions. Pairing two English learners allows them to practice communication skills and learn in a low-anxiety context. When a more proficient English speaker works with a less proficient English speaker, there is also an opportunity for the students to benefit from their roles as English teacher and learner.

Example
- » To begin exploration, students turn to their partners and each offers a prediction about an investigation or develops a concept; the teacher asks pairs to share unique predictions with the whole class.
- » During data analysis, students analyze charts and graphs and Pair-Share their interpretations (e.g., "I think this graph means that ...").
- » At the end of an investigation, students pair-share their conclusions.

SUMMARIZING

Purpose	Summarizing helps students understand complex information as they reorganize it for their own purposes. Summarizing can take place when students are engaged in problem solving or mathematics investigations, reading a text, or listening to a lecture as they seek to make sense of a body of new information. And because summaries identify key information, they help students review and study for tests.
Description	Summarizing requires students to comprehend and distill information into a parsimonious, synthesized form, in their own words. To effectively summarize information, the learner must recognize the main ideas, the expendable details, the illuminating details, and the terminology or academic language that is a crucial aspect of communicating the content.
	Note taking is closely related to summarizing, since to take effective notes, a student must determine what is most important and then state the information succinctly, in a way that will convey meaning for future use and review.
Use	Summarization at each chunk of new information helps students perform a mental task of moving meaningful chunks to long-term memory.
	The teacher begins teaching how to summarize and take notes by explaining the purpose and then modeling the process. Learning to summarize well is difficult, and so even secondary students can benefit from explicit practice, perhaps with the teacher providing writing prompts and templates that help students focus on the information that is most important. Novice English learners likely will need scaffolds such as sentence frames, graphic organizers, and illustrations. It may be helpful for English learners to complete summaries and notes with the support of small groups.
Examples	When students are expected to summarize in writing, English learners may be given activity sheets with sentence frames. Here are two examples, one for English learners at the *beginning/early intermediate* level and one for *intermediate* level. The underlined words are blank lines on the student's activity sheet.

Beginning/Early Intermediate English Learner

0 is a <u>natural</u> number.

0 is not a <u>counting</u> number.

The set of <u>integers</u> is {...-3, -2, -1, 0, 1, 2...}.

The set of <u>rational</u> numbers includes fractions.

<u>Irrational</u> numbers are non-terminating decimals that do not repeat.

Intermediate

The set of <u>natural</u> numbers is {0, 1, 2, 3, ...}.

The set of <u>counting</u> numbers is {1, 2, 3, ...}.

The set of <u>integers</u> is {...-3, -2, -1, 0, 1, 2...}.

<u>Rational</u> numbers include <u>natural numbers</u>, <u>counting numbers</u>, and <u>integers</u>.

<u>Irrational</u> numbers are <u>non-terminating</u> decimals that do not <u>repeat</u>.

RECIPROCAL TEACHING[7]

Purpose   Students learn four cognitive strategies by practicing them explicitly in small groups and teaching each other by assuming the roles of teacher and student.

Description   Reciprocal Teaching is an interactive, structured dialogue during the reading of text or mathematics tasks, or in small-group discussions while investigating a task or summarizing the solutions and strategies used. It involves four cognitive strategies — *questioning, summarizing, clarifying,* and *predicting.* These four processes are also core mathematical thinking processes, so Reciprocal Teaching capitalizes on investigation standards in mathematics. First, the teacher models the dialogue process; then students in pairs or small groups assume the roles of discussion leader (teacher role) and discussant(s) (student role).

Use   The teacher models one or more of the four processes with a short segment of the text or simple, brief task, then asks students to practice a cycle of Reciprocal Teaching in pairs or triads. The teacher gradually lengthens the reading segment or the complexity of the task. While students conduct Reciprocal Teaching, the teacher monitors and intervenes when necessary. Initially, the teacher provides intensive modeling and scaffolding and gradually fades out these prompts. For groups needing more assistance, the teacher continues to model. Summarizing is especially difficult for students to master. Additional practice, including practice with note taking, may be appropriate.

Word Walls and sample Sentence Frames can help English learners use academic language and participate in groups' Reciprocal Teaching conversations.

Example   The teacher gives student groups the following questions to answer during or after reading text about the definition, characteristics, and examples of prime numbers.

Question

After students read the selection, one student in the group asks another to answer a meaningful comprehension question provided by the teacher.

> "How many prime numbers are there?"

> "How many factors does a prime number have?"

Summarize

One student asks another to paraphrase the important points or concepts in the reading.

> "Please summarize in your own words what we have just read."

Clarify

Group members discuss any confusing aspects of the reading and try to make connections to knowledge they already have.

> "Is 1 a prime number? Its only factor is 1, so does that mean its only factor is 1 and itself?"

Predict

Students use new knowledge to make a conjecture.

> "My conjecture is that 2 is the only even prime number because all other even numbers have 2 as a factor."

> "I predict that prime numbers can be used to describe and compare other numbers."

ENDNOTES FOR CHAPTER 5

[1] The term was first used to describe parent-child talk by Wood, D.J., Bruner, J., & Ross, G. (1976). The role of tutoring in problem solving. *Journal of Child Psychology and Psychiatry* 17(2), 89–100.

[2] Scaffolding is discussed widely in education literature. The following sources are particularly germane to this presentation of scaffolding mathematics instruction for English learners:

Coggins, D., Kravin, D., Coates, G.D., & Carroll, M.D. (2007). *English language learners in the mathematics classroom*. Thousand Oaks, CA: Corwin Press.

Ellis, E.S., & Worthington, L.A. (2004). Executive summary of the research synthesis on effective teaching principles and the design of quality tools for educators. Accessed February 1, 2006, from http//idea.uoregon. edu/~ncite/documents/techrep/tech05.pdf.

Freeman, D., & Freeman, Y. (1988). Sheltered English instruction. *ERIC Digest* (ED301070). Washington, DC: ERIC Clearinghouse on Languages and Linguistics. Accessed March 3, 2006, from http://www.ericdigests.org/pre-9210/english.htm.

National Clearinghouse on Bilingual Education. (1987). Sheltered English: An approach to content area instruction for limited-English-proficient students. *Forum, 10*(6), 1–3.

Vygotsky, L. (1986). *Thought and language*. Ed. and trans. A. Kozulin. Cambridge, MA: Harvard University Press.

[3] Gibbons, P. (2002). *Scaffolding language, scaffolding learning*. Portsmouth, NH: Heinemann.

[4] See, for example, the resources that follow:

Marzano, R.J., Pickering, D.J., & Pollock, J.E. (2001). *Classroom instruction that works: Research-based strategies for increasing student achievement*. Alexandria, VA: Association for Supervision and Curriculum Development.

California Department of Education. (2000). *Strategic teaching and learning: Standards-based instruction to promote content literacy in grades four through twelve*. Sacramento: California Department of Education Press.

Herrell, A.L., & Jordan, M.L. (2003). *Fifty strategies for teaching English language learners*. Englewood Cliffs, NJ: Prentice Hall.

[5] Hill, J.D., & Flynn, K.M. (2006). *Classroom instruction that works with English language learners*. Alexandria, VA: Association for Supervision and Curriculum Development.

[6] To learn about Cornell style of note-taking, see http://coe.jmu.edu/learningtoolbox/cornellnotes.html, last accessed February 20, 2009.

[7] For the original research and definition of reciprocal teaching, see: Palincsar, A.S. (1986). Reciprocal teaching. In *Teaching reading as thinking*. Oak Brook, IL: North Central Regional Educational Laboratory.

For a review of all research, see: Rosenshine, B., & Meister, C. (1994). Reciprocal teaching: A review of the research. *Review of Educational Research, 64*(4), 479–530.

For a brief definition of the four components, see: http://www.ncrel.org/sdrs/areas/issues/students/atrisk/at6lk38.htm.

CHAPTER 6

Assessing English Learners

Mathematics teachers who focus on giving English learners equal access to the curriculum will also want to make sure that these students have a reasonable way to communicate what they are learning. Equal opportunity for English learners means scaffolding the assessment so that English learners can comprehend what is being asked, and scaffolding oral or written responses in order to support students in expressing their understanding of mathematics. Assessments must target mathematics standards, not language arts standards, so language errors are ignored for all students. Alternative assessments and accommodations (scaffolding strategies for assessment) can support English learners in understanding and expressing ideas in English.[1]

This chapter discusses how to select, modify, and administer good classroom assessments that inform a teacher about English learners' true understanding of mathematics content. The heart of this chapter describes a variety of accommodations that can make classroom assessments fair for English learners. These accommodations maintain a focus on the same content standards set for all students, while offering students different ways of performing on the assessment that respect their differences and yield accurate results. (Chapter 7 describes three lessons that integrate these accommodations during instruction.)

CLASSROOM ASSESSMENT

Assessing students at the end of each study unit or chapter — summative assessment — informs the teacher and student of final levels of accomplishment and allows the teacher to analyze results for groups of students, as well as for individuals. Information about what mathematics content was challenging for each student informs the teacher's decisions about how to modify the teaching strategies and activities for the next lesson or to offer program interventions such as tutoring. But how can the teacher greatly improve mathematics learning during the unit? Summative assessment is not enough. In support of summative assessment, formative assessment, particularly techniques to check for understanding[2] before the start of a lesson and repeatedly during a lesson, is the key to effective teaching and learning.

The National Research Council frames such assessment as the process of teaching scientifically:

> Teachers collect information about students' understanding almost continuously and make adjustments to their teaching on the basis of their interpretation of that information. They observe critical incidents in the classroom, formulate hypotheses about the causes of those incidents, question students to test their hypotheses, interpret students' responses, and adjust their teaching plans.[3]

In these terms, assessment allows the teacher to treat each lesson as an experiment: Predicting that certain strategies and activities will help students learn rigorous content; monitoring the effects of the lesson on student engagement and achievement; and analyzing the assessment data to make conclusions about teaching practices and materials.

Formative assessment can be a powerful teaching tool when teachers use the results to adjust their instructional strategies to reach all students in the classroom.[4] As Benjamin Bloom found, teachers using formative assessment dramatically narrowed the range of student achievement (test scores), and the average student in such classrooms outperformed 84 percent (instead of the expected 50 percent) of students in traditional classrooms where the teachers did not make instructional adjustments.[5] In other words, when teachers take the time to assess as they teach, and use the feedback, the process can result in more students mastering the lesson content.

The effective teacher uses a few quick and easy methods to survey what students do and do not understand during the course of a lesson and then tries different approaches as needed. Just as an ounce of prevention is worth a pound of cure, noticing early failures to comprehend key ideas and adjusting a lesson to fit student needs can prevent many failures at the end of the unit of study.

Three techniques to check for understanding during a lesson are gaining in popularity among elementary, middle school, and high school teachers:

» Hand gestures such as thumbs up (I agree, yes), thumbs to the side (I politely disagree, no), and flat hand over the head (I do not understand the question or comment);

» Color-coded cards — agree, disagree, don't understand; and

» White boards on which each student quickly illustrates or writes a brief answer and holds it up for the teacher to see.

These techniques can be used to respond to what the teacher or another student says. Asking all students to quickly show agreement or disagreement with another student's answer or comment engages all students in listening critically to one another and widens the conversation from teacher–student to teacher–student–students. Students easily adapt to these techniques, and the process is both fast and comfortable. And the teacher can take immediate action based on what the students reveal. For example, a concept about which many students signal confusion indicates to the teacher the need to take a different approach; if a smaller group of students signal that they do not understand, the teacher may convene them for more specific instruction while other students move into an independent activity.

Monitoring students while they are working individually or in small groups can be considered checking for understanding. The teacher is able to observe many students and provide cues or other teaching techniques to guide individual students in their learning activities. When many students are confused, the teacher may stop the independent work and conduct direct instruction to clarify concepts or the learning activity itself. This is what makes a good teacher really effective — planning a good lesson and then making it better during instruction so all students can be successful.

Checking for understanding not only helps the teacher adjust a lesson, it also provides feedback to students about what they do know and what they need to learn. Getting informative feedback[6] from the teacher throughout a lesson helps students assume control and responsibility for their learning, and adjust learning as needed. The mathematics teacher can include feedback about English language conventions and verbal expression while checking for understanding. For example, if a beginning English learner responds, "Octagon have eight side," the teacher provides implicit corrective feedback while acknowledging the correct mathematics answer: "Yes, octagons have eight sides." This can occur orally or in writing depending on whether the student is speaking or writing answers.

ASSESSMENT ACCOMMODATIONS FOR ENGLISH LEARNERS

Accommodations are meant to elicit the most accurate information about what students know and can do, without giving them an unfair advantage over students who do not receive the accommodations. All students are diverse test takers as well as diverse learners. Some may have pronounced learning strengths in certain modalities, such as visual or aural, or they may have assessment preferences that influence their ability to show what they truly know. For English learners, an additional consideration is the challenge they face to perform in English. The more alternatives an assessment includes, the more accurate the test results are likely to be for a range of students.

Figure 6.1 describes common testing accommodations that teachers may use in their classrooms with English learners. It is assumed that testing is in English only. Some accommodations address how a test is administered; others address the test instrument and task options. The closer an English learner is to the beginning ELD level, the more scaffolding of the student's interaction with the test will be required.

Two interrelated accommodations that are effective in reducing the assessment performance gap between English learners and native English speakers are revised test directions and revised test items.[7] Just as the syntax of test items can be revised to reduce complexity (and still measure students' knowledge of the mathematics construct at the same level of difficulty), vocabulary can be changed without dumbing down the content, as well. Ensuring that key vocabulary and syntax of test directions and items are taught and practiced during instruction avoids oversimplifying test language. For example, during testing a teacher can ask for "synonyms" instead of "words with the same meaning," as long as students have become quite familiar with synonyms during instruction. Teachers need to ensure their students are familiar with non-mathematics vocabulary on tests, as well as with mathematics terms. When contextual wording is used in test items, teachers should consider changing less culturally familiar words and phrases to words and phrases that reflect more familiar cultural experiences (e.g., from "fish in an aquarium" to "students on the playground").

ACCOMMODATIONS BY TYPE OF ASSESSMENT

The particular accommodations the teacher decides to use with English learners will vary by the type of assessment, as well as by the student's level of English proficiency. Several kinds of assessments that teachers commonly use are described below, along with suggestions to accommodate English learners.

FIGURE 6.1. Test Accommodations for Use With English Learners

Test Accommodation	Purpose or Use
Extra Time	Provide extra time for English learners to read and understand test questions. They have extra thinking to do simply to understand and respond to a question in English.
Word Walls, Glossaries	Provide word walls created during instruction for reference during assessment so English learners can more easily communicate conceptual thinking. Allow English learners at appropriate ELD levels to use glossaries (except when testing vocabulary, of course).
Notes In Primary Language	When students are allowed to use notes during an assessment, allow English learners to refer to notes they made in their primary language. In this way the teacher makes it more likely that students can produce, in English, answers that they know in their primary language.
Models and Rubrics	Provide models of expected student work, particularly for students who have not previously produced this kind of product. Preview the scoring guide or rubric that will be used to judge the work. Previewing models and explaining rubrics before or during instruction helps students understand lesson and assessment objectives.
Revised Test Directions	Some test directions can be much more difficult to understand than the concepts measured. Revise test directions to reduce linguistic complexity. Read directions aloud and rephrase them as necessary to be sure English learners know what they are expected to do. Simplify test directions as much as possible. For example, segment multi-step directions if possible, stating one step at a time and allowing for student response between steps. When responses cannot be segmented, have students use the directions as a checklist for reviewing that they have completed all parts of the task.
Revised Test Items	Revise test items to reduce linguistic complexity. Ensure that English learners encounter in a test the same key words and phrases that were used during instruction. Increase students' opportunity to understand the questions by providing synonyms or additional context for key ideas.
Oral Responses	Communicating through writing can be very challenging for English learners, especially when anxiety is high during an assessment. Allow novice English learners to give oral responses while the rest of the class completes a written test. (Out of range of the rest of the class, prompt students individually and scaffold the conversation as necessary to elicit meaningful responses.) Provide sentence frames for English learners who need support with open-ended questions and ask them to attempt written answers; then prompt students orally to give them an opportunity to clarify written answers that are ambiguous or confusing.
Illustrations, Graphic Organizers	Allow students to express ideas with labeled drawings, diagrams, or graphic organizers. Follow up by asking students to give oral explanations, written open-ended responses, or demonstrations.
Hands-on Activities	Have students perform a demonstration, activity, or investigation, and describe or explain their actions and thinking processes. For example, students might cycle through various assessment task stations in the classroom, responding to the problem or question posed at each station. Have students who can write brief answers do so, and orally prompt English learners as needed.
Language Conventions	Ignore errors in language conventions in order to focus on students' understanding of mathematics content. The time for corrective feedback of oral or written responses is during instruction. Expect *beginning* and *early intermediate* English learners to make many errors as they struggle to communicate meaning.
Small Groups	Administer a test separately to a small group of English learners if it helps to lower their anxiety (students still individually complete the test). Use prompts and scaffolds with individuals in the group and allow oral responses as appropriate to elicit students' best performance.

Source: Carr, J., Sexton, U., & Lagunoff, R. (2007). *Making Science Accessible to English Learners: A Guidebook for Teachers*. San Francisco, CA: WestEd.

Cloze Test

Cloze tests are similar to Sentence Frames. They require students to fill in the blanks in sentences (e.g., A quadrilateral has ___ sides). A word bank may be provided, but it should include extra words and/or allow for words to be used more than once. The point is to reduce student guessing so that the teacher is fairly certain what students do and do not know, and can confidently plan what to teach next. When constructing or revising Cloze test items, teachers should:

> » Ensure that all words in a sentence are familiar to English learners so that the assessment is testing only students' knowledge of the intended terms — those represented with blanks.

> » For *beginning* and *early intermediate* students, modify sentences to be as simple as possible and to help students with the reading.

Multiple-Choice Test

Multiple-choice tests can be very difficult for English learners since the test items are typically very succinct — with little context to help English learners figure out what an item means. Teachers may need to support English learners by rephrasing and providing context clues for certain test items. Suggested supports include:

> » Spend a little time teaching test-taking skills, particularly related to mathematics. If some test items require students to pick the "best" answer, ensure that English learners understand and have had experience with this type of item. Let them know that there may be answers that are partially correct but just not as good as the "most correct" or "best" answer.

> » Limit the number of items, especially items with long statements, to avoid student fatigue.

> » Eliminate items with answer choices such as "None of the above" and "A and B" to avoid confusion and cognitive overload.

> » Make sure item stems and answer choices are written in the simplest, most straightforward wording possible. Highlight key words (in bold, underline, or all capital letters), particularly negatives such as "not," so English learners do not miss them.

For multiple-choice tests that base items on illustrations, graphs, or tables, the following tips are helpful for all learners and are especially important to avoid confusing English learners.[8]

> » Make sure illustrations are accurate and clear and include appropriate scales when relevant.

> » Use an illustration as a reference for multiple questions. English learners will benefit from the familiar context.

> » Be sure the labels on the illustration match those embedded in item prompts.

> » Limit the steps necessary to interpret information from an illustration, graph, or table.

» When possible, select contexts that are familiar to students or that relate to their backgrounds and experiences.

Short-Answer Test

Students can respond orally or in writing to test items calling for a phrase or up to a few sentences. When applicable, students may be encouraged to draw illustrations or to create or fill in simple graphic organizers (e.g., to show relationships among polygons), organizing their thoughts before answering aloud or in writing. Short-answer tests can be structured to provide sentence starters and function words to connect ideas, with the amount of support matching students' ELD levels.

» For *beginning* English learners, conduct the test orally, individually, and out of range of the rest of the class. Use visual supports without giving away answers, particularly for English learners whose strong modality is visual or spatial.

» For *early intermediate* English learners, conduct the test orally or orally prompt for certain items that students may have had trouble answering in writing. Word Walls and Sentence Frames support students to communicate what they know.

» *Intermediate* English learners can answer in writing but may need supports such as Word Walls and Sentence Frames.

Written Performance Tasks

The writing students do in mathematics varies across types, purposes, and products. For example, students write expository, descriptive, analytic, and technical responses or reports. They write for purposes such as exemplifying, describing phenomena, raising questions, clarifying, and supporting ideas. And they create different types of products such as notes, portfolios, data charts, reports, essays, and logs.

Students need explicit teaching about the purpose and form of each type of writing. Such instruction by the mathematics teacher can be supported with collaboration from the English language arts or ELD teacher. For all students, models should be a key feature of writing instruction. Models should be discussed with students and available for them to investigate and refer to. Graphic organizers can be used to help students make visual sense of their thinking. Word Walls might also be readily available to English learners.

The teacher might elicit student writing at all ELD levels but with different expectations depending on a student's English proficiency:

» *Beginning* level English learners may give brief oral answers and attempt to write a few simple phrases or sentences.

» *Early intermediate* level English learners may write a few simple sentences followed by oral responses prompted by the teacher.

» *Intermediate* level English learners may write sentences and short paragraphs and clarify them orally as prompted by the teacher.

» *Early advanced* and *advanced* English learners might be expected to produce paragraphs and compositions; the teacher is aware that language convention errors are still natural as students continue learning English grammar and idioms.

Figure 6.2 is an example of a written mathematics assessment that gives English learners an opportunity to express their understanding at varying levels of language development. The assessment content is aligned with content standards relating to points on a coordinate plane. Students approach the topic through three types of scaffolded items: identifying independent and dependent variables on a graph, describing the meaning of points on the graph, and drawing conclusions from the graph in an open-ended writing task.

The English language requirements of this sample assessment item are appropriate for English learners at intermediate and higher levels of proficiency, as well as students whose first language is English. The scaffolds in the item are both conceptual (addressing increasingly challenging concepts) and linguistic (requiring increasingly advanced language skills). The assessment includes the following language components:

> An illustration with labels to serve as reference for the entire assessment;

> Two items not requiring writing;

> Three items that require short sentences; and

> An open-ended question requiring one or two written sentences.

To differentiate the assessment item for English learners at *beginning* and *early intermediate* levels, the assessment item could be modified to include more support. Such support might include:

> Rephrasing the directions (e.g., "Explain using words what point A (75, 12) means.")

> Providing an embedded example response (e.g., "If your heart is beating 75 times per minute, then you are taking 12 breaths per minute.")

> Offering the option of Cloze-response prompts in the form of sentence frames with key vocabulary highlighted in bold letters (e.g., "If your heart is **beating** 130 times **per minute**, then you are taking ___ **breaths per minute**.")

> Prompting the English learner to respond orally

> Providing a word wall that includes key vocabulary (e.g., "graph," "compare," "variable," "point," "per minute," "related," "independent," "dependent," "beating," "breaths")

> Segmenting a question with multiple parts into several separate questions or bulleted statements

Oral Presentations

Beginning or *early intermediate* English learners should not be required to present formal oral reports in mainstream classrooms; modified presentations might be appropriate in sheltered classrooms (where all students are English learners). *Intermediate* students might give oral presentations with teacher support as needed (e.g., prompting, rephrasing to achieve a coherent response), if the students agree, and classroom conditions are risk-free and supportive. Multimedia and use of technology such as PowerPoint, where visuals are blended with brief text, can support English learners as they orally present their reports.

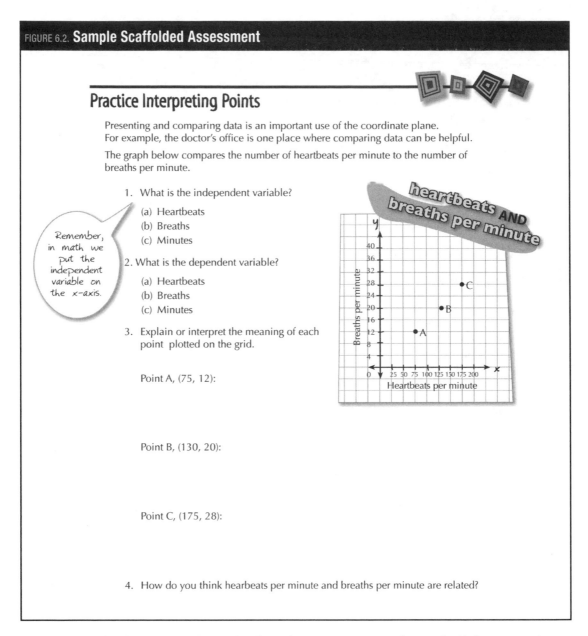

FIGURE 6.2. **Sample Scaffolded Assessment**

Practice Interpreting Points

Presenting and comparing data is an important use of the coordinate plane. For example, the doctor's office is one place where comparing data can be helpful.

The graph below compares the number of heartbeats per minute to the number of breaths per minute.

1. What is the independent variable?

   (a) Heartbeats
   (b) Breaths
   (c) Minutes

2. What is the dependent variable?

   (a) Heartbeats
   (b) Breaths
   (c) Minutes

Remember, in math we put the independent variable on the x-axis.

3. Explain or interpret the meaning of each point plotted on the grid.

   Point A, (75, 12):

   Point B, (130, 20):

   Point C, (175, 28):

4. How do you think hearbeats per minute and breaths per minute are related?

Source: Presented with permission of WestEd and It's About Time; appears in the *Aim for Algebra* program (in press). Accessed October 22, 2008, from http://www.its-about-time.com/aim/aim.html.

When English learners work in cooperative groups on a task culminating in an oral presentation, reporting in front of the class should be assigned to other students, while English learners are gradually prepared to participate more fully in oral presentations.

Performance Assessments

Performance assessments require students to complete a task that can range from a set of short duration, limited scope tasks, to a complex project that continues for many days.[9]

INTEGRATING INSTRUCTION AND ASSESSMENT

In standards-based lesson planning, also called *backwards mapping*,[10] the teacher first selects specific content standards as the lesson objectives, choosing a few of the most important or essential standards to discuss with students so they know to focus on these. As the lesson progresses, the teacher remains aware of the full complement of standards and makes connections to them as appropriate.

Second, the teacher selects a good summative assessment that emphasizes those essential standards and then builds in accommodations for English learners. The teacher is aware of the test format, and the vocabulary, knowledge, and skills required to answer the questions and follow the test directions. If possible, the teacher offers alternatives, knowing that diverse learners also prefer diverse ways to show what they have learned. The teacher asks several questions in evaluating an assessment:

» Does the assessment truly measure (at least) the essential standards?

» What will proficient performance on this assessment look like?

» Do the accommodations for English learners really measure the mathematics content standards at a reasonable level of rigor, similar to that required of other students?

Third, the teacher plans learning activities so that all students have equal opportunity to learn the content and practice the skills. Equal opportunity means that diverse learning activities are presented to students because they have diverse styles, interests, and levels of learning. Visual learners, for example, have graphic organizers and other visual means to access content, but they also experience other modalities so that they become well-rounded learners and appreciate a variety of styles within the classroom. Reading materials are geared to students' various reading levels. Students are able to choose from alternative tasks, which leads them to become more responsible for their own learning. In selecting the learning activities, the teacher reflects on each and asks whether it helps students understand the essential standards and prepares them for the assessment.

Fourth, the teacher plans instructional strategies and builds in differentiation, or scaffolds, for English learners at different ELD levels. Instruction is multimodal, perhaps focusing on a particular mode at one time and reviewing what was learned by focusing on another mode. Accommodations such as use of graphic organizers that appear in the assessment are part of the instructional strategies. The teacher evaluates the instructional strategies in light of whether they try to reach and respect the diversity of learners in the classroom, and are linked to the assessment strategies.

Last, the teacher helps students connect the dots by reviewing the entire unit lesson plan. What is taught is assessed. There must be a clear connection among the standards, assessment, student activities, and teaching strategies. If not, the teacher amends the lesson plan. During instruction, the teacher uses frequent formative assessments, checking for understanding and using the feedback to quickly adjust the lesson and try other strategies.

SHARING RESULTS AND IDEAS

A teacher can learn much from assessments or test results but still miss some things or not know how to help some students who are struggling. Collaborating with other teachers to evaluate student work or analyze test results can enhance both student and teacher learning.[11]

The shared evaluation of student work might start with a trusted colleague and expand to departmental study teams. These sessions enable teachers to become more skilled at evaluating student work by giving them the opportunity to review and analyze a larger sample of work than that of their own students. By sharing results, teachers can also evaluate their individual programs and instructional practices in comparison with those of their peers.

While analyzing student results together, collaborating teachers also consider what they might do better the next time. They take a hard look at the results for lower-scoring students to determine whether the test was accurate and fair for these students. They also explore different teaching strategies and learning activities that might better help these students as a group, and they share insights about individual students. This kind of embedded professional development is highly relevant to teachers and can produce valuable results for students.

ENDNOTES FOR CHAPTER 6

[1] Trumbull, E., & Farr, B. (2005). *Language and learning: What teachers need to know.* Norwood, MA: Christopher Gordon. See chapter 7, Language and Assessment.

[2] For a complete discussion and many techniques, see Fisher, D., & Frey, N. (2007). *Checking for understanding: Formative assessment techniques for your classroom.* Alexandria, VA: Association for Supervision and Curriculum Development.

[3] National Research Council. (1996). *National Science Education Standards* (p. 87). Washington, DC: National Academy Press. Retrieved February 26, 2006, from http://www.nap.edu/catalog/4962.html.

[4] Black, P., & William, D. (1998). Inside the black box: Raising standards through classroom assessment. *Phi Delta Kappan, 80*(2), 139–149.

[5] Bloom, B. (1984). The search for methods of group instruction as effective as one-to-one tutoring. *Educational Leadership, 41*(8), 4–17.

[6] Brookhart, S.M. (2008). How to give effective feedback to your students. Alexandria, VA: Association for Supervision and Curriculum Development.

[7] Abedi, J. (2002 Spring). Assessment and accommodations of English language learners: Issues, concerns, and recommendations. *Journal of School Improvement, 3*(1). Accessed 14 October 2008, from http://www.icsac.org/jsi/2002v3i1/assessment. Abedi offers examples of test items that can be simplified at http://www.ncela.gwu.edu/spotlight/LEP/Presentations07/USDPaternOct07.pdf (last accessed October 14, 2008).

[8] Sexton, U., & Solano-Flores, G. (2002 April). *Cultural validity in assessment: A cross-cultural study of the interpretation of mathematics and science test items.* Paper presented at the annual meeting of the American Educational Research Association, New Orleans.

[9] *Performance Assessment Links in Math* is an online, standards-based, resource bank of tasks indexed via the National Council of Teachers of Mathematics (NCTM). Accessed November 12, 2008, from http://palm.sri.com/.

[10] Wiggins, G., & McTighe, J. (1998). *Understanding by design.* Alexandria, VA: Association for Supervision and Curriculum Development.

[11] Darling-Hammond, L., & Richardson, N. (2009). Teacher learning: What matters? *Educational Leadership, 66*(5), 46–55.
Loucks-Horsley, S., Love, N., Stiles, K.E., Mundry, S., & Hewson, P.W. (2003). *Designing professional development for teachers of science and mathematics.* Thousand Oaks, CA: Corwin Press.

CHAPTER 7
Applying Strategies in the Classroom

The purpose of this guidebook is to present and illustrate a practical, integrated approach to supporting English learners in the mathematics classroom. The previous three chapters presented examples of individual strategies; this chapter models the integration of these strategies within a mathematics lesson. Three classroom scenarios are presented as examples of applying and integrating vocabulary development, as discussed in chapter 4, and content scaffolding as described in chapter 5. In "Graphing Cellphone Charges," a teacher describes how she uses the Academic Language Skills (ALS) chart to differentiate instruction for three levels of English learners. "Engaging with Hexagons" (page 95) illustrates how a teacher modifies an activity sheet to support language development. "Express Your Age" (page 97) highlights the use of modeling and formative assessment techniques.

GRAPHING CELLPHONE CHARGES

Class: Algebra I

Activity: Graphing an equation

Instructional strategies: Differentiating instruction for diverse learners using the Academic Language Skills (ALS) chart for grades 9–12

After identifying Algebra I standards that are appropriate for this lesson, I consider the key concepts, tasks, and skills that may be required of my students. I specifically note that this lesson requires them to communicate their understanding of how to solve problems and how to make predictions from data graphed on a coordinate plane. I also consider the kinds of learning experiences and activities that will engage all students in the lesson and help them develop their academic language.

Working in pairs, students will predict cell phone charges for calls of different lengths, graphing an equation based on ordered pairs in a table. Students will show their work on paper and respond orally to my questions as I monitor their understanding of the work. (Figure 7.1 presents the student activity sheet.) The English learners in my class will use language appropriate to their level. The short sentences are at the readability level of English learners at the *intermediate* level or some at the *early intermediate* level. I will pair *beginning* and other *early intermediate* English learners with more English proficient students to read and complete the activity sheet.

After planning my instructional strategies for the whole class, I refer to the grades 9–12 ALS chart to consider how I should tailor strategies to fit my English learners. A thread that runs through all my lessons is my attempt to always support what I say — especially during direct instruction — with visuals, such as a Word Wall, graphic organizer, or pictures and illustrations. When I review the ALS chart, the activity sheet for students, and the instructional strategies I plan to use, I realize that I can combine my *early intermediate* and *intermediate* English learners for

FIGURE 7.1. **Graphing Cell Phone Charges Activity**

Graphing equations can also help us answer questions about the future and make predictions.

Joe's cell phone company has a base charge of 20 cents per call and then, a charge of 10 cents per minute of calling time. So for a **1**-minute call he would pay 20¢ plus **1**(10¢) or 30 cents. For a **3**-minute call he would pay 20¢ plus **3**(10¢) or 50 cents.

20¢ + 1(10¢) = 30¢
base charge · 1 minute charge · total cost

Joe wants to predict the charges for calls of different lengths and decides to make a graph.

Using "t" as the time of the call in minutes and "c" as the total cost of the call in cents,

- Label the horizontal axis "Time of call in minutes".
- Label the vertical axis "Cost of the call in cents".
- Label the scale for each axis. (Hint: To label the c-axis, skip count by 10s.)
- Fill in the table for calls of 1 minute, 2 minutes, 5 minutes, and 9 minutes.
- Graph the ordered pairs in the table.

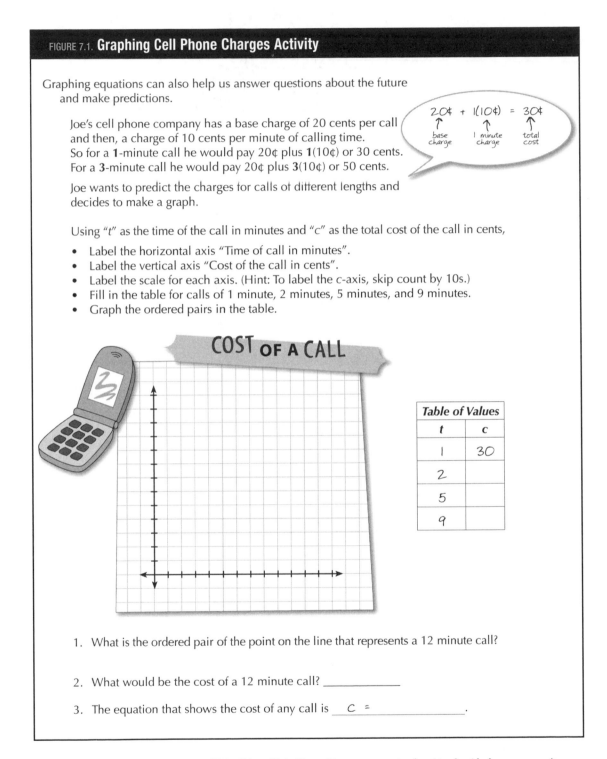

COST OF A CALL

Table of Values

t	c
1	30
2	
5	
9	

1. What is the ordered pair of the point on the line that represents a 12 minute call?

2. What would be the cost of a 12 minute call? _____

3. The equation that shows the cost of any call is ___ $C =$ _____ .

Source: Presented with permission of WestEd and It's About Time; appears in the *Aim for Algebra* program (in press). Accessed October 22, 2008, from http://www.its-about-time.com/aim/aim.html.

some skills instruction. The chart (Figure 7.2) below shows my modification of the general ALS chart for this lesson.

FIGURE 7.2. **Example of Grades 9–12 ALS Chart Applied to a Mathematics Lesson**			
AL Skills	**Early Intermediate**	**Intermediate**	**Early Advanced**
Listen with Understanding	Use an activity sheet with simple directions; orally state the directions; reinforce for *advanced beginners* who are paired with more English proficient students.		Use same activity sheet and hear directions presented orally.
Use Academic Language	Use key words and informal definitions from the word wall during group activities and class discussion. Target words for this task: *graph, scale, linear equation, horizontal, vertical, axis, ordered pairs* for all students; *base charge, per,* and *predict* for English learners.		Use expanded vocabulary and more detailed sentences. Use word parts and glossary to define new words.
Ask and Answer Questions	Orally ask and briefly answer factual questions.	Orally ask and answer factual questions.	Ask and answer any questions, orally and in writing.
Take Notes	Use template created for all students (very little writing is required).		
Read with Comprehension	Read activity sheet with assistance (paired with higher level student)	Read activity sheet independently; directions are sentences at students' reading level.	

To build the Listen with Understanding skill, I will orally review the bulleted directions on students' activity sheets, pointing to the same items on an activity sheet transparency projected on the wall, and check for understanding with my *advanced beginner* and perhaps *intermediate* English learners. Written directions are in simple sentences that my *advanced beginner* students can read. *Advanced beginners'* understanding of oral and written directions will be reinforced because they are paired with more English proficient students to complete the activity. There is very little note taking for this activity, so sentence starters are not needed to support my English learners. To address the Read with Comprehension skills, my *advanced beginners* will be paired with more English literate students. These texts are brief and simple enough for my *intermediate* and higher level English learners to understand.

As I launch into the first part of the lesson, I want to both engage students' interest and check for what they already know about the context of cell phone charges, and about the mathematical ideas needed to predict phone charges and compare plans offered by various phone companies. During this introduction, students will share what they already know about cell phone charges, criteria for selecting the best carrier, and other related topics. I will record on the board all contributions from students, and enter ideas that are pertinent to the upcoming lesson in the K column of a KWL+ chart.

During lesson planning, I identified seven target words or terms that might be new to all students, and three words that many of my English learners may not know, to help them understand and discuss concepts. (See Figure 7.2 for a list of the words.) I will introduce new words in the context of the lesson and add them to a Word Wall chart as they are used. As a quick review and check for understanding during the lesson, I will assign two words from the word wall to each table group (four students per table) and ask them to define the word by using an informal definition, an example sentence, or illustration. I will use Think-Pair-Share to allow each student up to a minute to think of a way to define an assigned word. Then pairs with the same word will share their definitions, and select one definition to share with one of the pairs who were assigned the other word. I will invite groups to volunteer definitions and I'll enter those that are accurate next to the words on the word wall. I will tell students that I expect them to use these target words as they talk with partners during the activity that follows.

In my planning, I also noticed the term "c-axis," which I anticipate will confuse students as they reason about the activity. I will Think Aloud about how I figure out what "c-axis" means in this particular activity, modeling what good readers do to determine the meaning of a word or phrase in context. For example, "The c-axis must be one of the axes on the graph. I read that c represents the cost of a call, and the vertical axis shows the cost of a call. So the c-axis must refer to the vertical axis."

Before students begin to work on the activity sheet for the *investigate* phase, I'll ask them to explain the purpose of the task and to restate the directions. To keep all students' attention as I check for understanding, after a student responds I'll ask the class to agree or disagree by using a respectful thumbs-up or thumbs-down gesture. Next, to check for understanding and to ensure students can identify the question in a task or word problem, I will read aloud the three questions below the picture of a graph (What is the ordered pair for a 12-minute call? What is the cost for a 12-minute call? and What is the equation for the cost of any call?). I will then ask students what they want to know, and write appropriate responses to the three questions, in students' words, in the W column of my KWL chart.

As individuals and pairs of students complete the activity sheet, I will encourage them to use the new vocabulary words (see Figure 7.2 above) as they discuss their ideas with each other and me. Most students in the class will work alone on this activity sheet. For other lessons I will have students work in pairs or small groups so that peers reinforce concepts and each student has an opportunity to practice listening and speaking skills that target mathematical language.

I'll also ask students questions that require them to make conclusions or reflect on the lesson, to give them practice expressing their mathematical thinking orally. I'll ask about their strategies before I ask for answers to the task's questions. This order helps to emphasize problem-solving strategies and avoids the "Who's right?" discussion. Again, I will use Think-Pair-Share to involve all students and create a comfortable situation in which English learners can express their thinking before whole-class discussion. My questions to elicit conclusions and reflection will be:

» Restate what you were asked to do.

» How did you decide what you could to do to find the solution?

>> What was your solution?

>> How did your solution answer the question?

ENGAGING WITH HEXAGONS

Class: Integrated Mathematics I

Activity: Writing an explicit rule for a pattern

Instructional strategies: Modifying activity instructions to allow English learners to focus on the mathematical concepts

To engage students in the content of this activity, the teacher asks them to describe patterns they are familiar with, particularly patterns involving geometric figures. The teacher is prepared either to show students' samples she's gathered of geometric patterns, or to ask students to draw their own sample patterns on the board. She focuses on establishing students' understanding of the vocabulary word "pattern." After eliciting students' prior knowledge and experiences, the teacher gives them the following activity sheet (Figure 7.3), which shows linear patterns of a geometric figure (a hexagon) and asks students to determine the recursive and explicit rules for creating the pattern.

To further introduce the content of the page, the teacher briefly discusses the characteristics of hexagons with students (specifically that they have 6 sides). Together, the teacher and students use pattern blocks or sticks to build the pattern already shown on the page. She discusses the way the hexagons are put together so that they have one shared side, and explains that students will be investigating a mathematical pattern by counting the number of edges and the number of shared sides in each of the hexagon figures. (Note: In this activity, the hexagons are regular hexagons, so the class might also discuss that the sides are all the same length. Because the activity focuses on the number of sides, and not the lengths of the sides, this is not a necessary point for students to recognize before investigating the activity.)

When the teacher reviewed the activity sheet before distributing it to students, she realized that the wording of instructions might be frustrating for English learners. To decrease the emphasis on written English, she changed complex directions into simple sentences or sentences with single steps, and controlled word choice. The mathematical complexity of the activity stays the same in the modified directions and questions. Figure 7.4 presents the activity sheet's original directions and questions in the left column, and the teacher's modified directions and questions in the right column. The teacher gives the modified activity sheet to English learners at the *beginning* and *early intermediate* levels of proficiency.

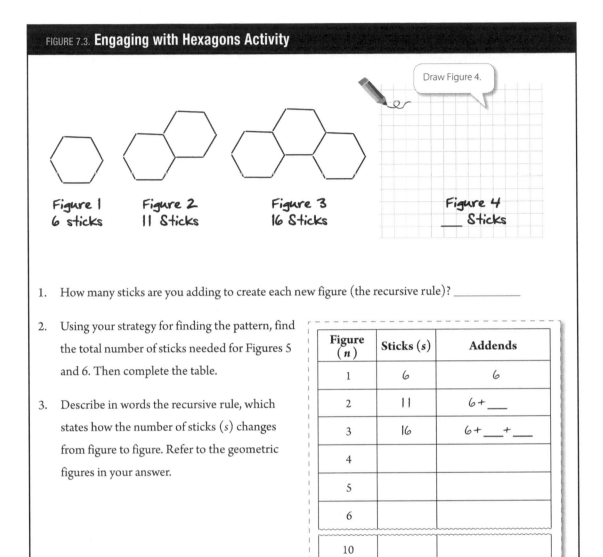

FIGURE 7.3. Engaging with Hexagons Activity

Draw Figure 4.

Figure 1
6 sticks

Figure 2
11 Sticks

Figure 3
16 Sticks

Figure 4
___ Sticks

1. How many sticks are you adding to create each new figure (the recursive rule)? _____

2. Using your strategy for finding the pattern, find the total number of sticks needed for Figures 5 and 6. Then complete the table.

3. Describe in words the recursive rule, which states how the number of sticks (s) changes from figure to figure. Refer to the geometric figures in your answer.

Figure (n)	Sticks (s)	Addends
1	6	6
2	11	6+ ___
3	16	6+ ___ + ___
4		
5		
6		
10		

4. Using algebraic notation, write an explicit rule that describes the pattern of growth for these figures. Describe your rule by referring to the geometric figures.

Use n to represent the figure number and s to represent the total number of sticks.

$S =$

5. Use your rule to show the total number of sticks needed for Figure 10. Enter your answer in the table.

Source: Presented with permission of WestEd and It's About Time; appears in the *Aim for Algebra* program (in press). Accessed October 22, 2008, from http://www.its-about-time.com/aim/aim.html.

FIGURE 7.4. **Directions for Hexagon Activity**

Original Directions	Modified Directions
1. How many sticks are you adding to create each new figure (the *recursive* rule)?	1. How many sticks did you add to create Figure 4? ___ (This is a clue to the *recursive* rule.)
2. Using your strategy for finding the pattern, find the total number of sticks needed for Figures 5 and 6. Then complete the table.	2. How many sticks are needed for Figure 5? How many sticks are needed for Figure 6? Write your answers in the table. Think about how you found the number of sticks.
3. Describe in words the *recursive* rule, which states how the number of sticks (s) changes from figure to figure. Refer to the geometric figures in your answer.	3. Use words to describe how the number of sticks grows from figure to figure. This is the *recursive* rule. Draw Figure 7 of the hexagon pattern to support your answer.
4. Using algebraic notation, write an *explicit* rule that describes the pattern of growth for these figures. Describe your rule by referring to the geometric figures.	4. Write the *explicit* rule using algebraic notation to describe the pattern.
5. Use your rule to show the total number of sticks needed for Figure 10. Enter your answer in the table.	5. Use your rule to compute the number of sticks for Figure 10. Be sure to use algebraic notation. Write your answer in the table.

As students complete the activity sheet, the teacher circulates and supports students who are struggling with either the mathematics or the language on the activity sheet. The teacher knows that students may think about the task in different ways, and she encourages all students to express their thoughts in any way they can.

EXPRESS YOUR AGE

Class: Pre-algebra

Activity: Writing algebraic expressions

Instructional strategies: Integrating visuals into a mathematical activity while modeling mathematical thinking and incorporating feedback from formative assessment

A pre-algebra teacher, Armando, uses this lesson to help students extend their understanding of numerical expressions to understanding algebraic expressions. Students initially represent information about changes in their age using only numbers. Following the steps in this activity (see Figure 7.5), they learn to represent changes in age with numbers and variables, thereby creating algebraic expressions to represent an unknown age. Specifically, students write numerical expressions to describe changes to a particular age. They then write algebraic expressions to describe the same changes, but to an unknown age.

FIGURE 7.5. **Express Your Age Activity**

Express Your Age

1. What is your age now? _____

2. How old will you be two years from now? _____

3. How old will you be ten years from now? _____

4. What is twice your age? _____

5. What is half your age? _____

6. In how many years will you be 50? _____

Nora and Max

What if we don't know someone's age and want to ask some questions?

Let **n** represent Nora's present age in years.

EXAMPLE
EXAMPLE
1. What is Nora's age now? _____ n _____

2. How old will Nora be two years from now? _____ $n + 2$ _____

3. How old will she be ten years from now? _____

THINK
How are questions 6 and 7 different?

4. What is twice Nora's current age? _____

5. What is half Nora's age? _____

6. How old will Nora be 50 years from now? _____

7. In how many years will she be 50 years old? _____

Let **m** represent Max's present age in years.

EXAMPLE
EXAMPLE
8. What is the sum of Nora's and Max's ages now? _____ $n + m$ _____

9. What is the sum of Nora's and Max's ages ten years from now? _____

Source: Presented with permission of WestEd and It's About Time; appears in the *Aim for Algebra* program (in press). Accessed October 22, 2008, from http://www.its-about-time.com/aim/aim.html.

Armando determines mathematical goals for this lesson and also identifies several language goals. The lesson requires students to respond in a numerical or symbolic form to phrases written in words. Understanding the meaning of the word phrases may be especially challenging for English learners. For example, " How old will Nora be 10 years from now?" and "In how many years will you be 50?" may be difficult for English learners to understand. Furthermore, there are no equal signs in expressions, so none are necessary for representing the ages. Each expression represents the age described. Armando also decides to focus throughout the lesson on helping students correctly state mathematical expressions, such as by saying "the quantity of n" when referring to the variable n.

Armando begins the lesson by modeling responses to the set of questions at the top of the page, using his own age. He also uses a horizontal number line as a time line, placing key words or phrases to the right or left of his age. He encourages all students to answer the questions and participate in the class discussion by: (a) having pairs or small groups discuss answers before eliciting responses, or (b) having all students use a respectful thumbs-up or thumbs-down gesture to agree or disagree with a student's response to the teacher.

Armando reads aloud the first question, "What is your age now?" He asks a student to guess his age. He points to the number line and says, "Now, I am 44 years old." He writes, "Now, I am" next to 44. He reads aloud question 2, "How old *will* you be two years *from now*?" (He emphasizes the italicized words.) Armando points to the time line as he asks, "Where should I write 'will be...from now,' left or right of 44 on the time line?" He asks students to respond with a thumbs-up gesture to mean greater than 44 or thumbs-down gesture to mean less than 44. Armando watches the responses of his *beginning* English learners in particular to check their understanding of the phrases "will be __ years old __ years from now."

Armando repeats question 2, "How old will you be two years from now?" He waits a few seconds to allow all students a chance to think. A student responds, "46." Armando asks students to gesture thumbs up or down if they agree or disagree. Armando models a complete sentence as feedback, "Yes, I will be 46 years old." Armando asks students for a mathematical expression that describes how they found the age. After eliciting at least one response, he writes "44 + 2" next to 46 on the number line. This reinforces the idea of how to create an expression to represent a quantity, and it serves as an introduction to creating expressions with a variable (n). Throughout the discussion, Armando scaffolds English learners' understanding of what's said, using visual representations such as the number line.

Armando goes to the overhead projector, asks for the age and a mathematical expression for question 3, again giving feedback and writing the expression on the transparency. After asking for responses from students, he says, "The mathematical expression is 44 + 10. In 10 years, I will be 54 years old," to again reinforce the expression representing the quantity.

Armando reads aloud question 4, "What is *twice* your age?" He asks, "Does 'twice' mean 'greater than' or 'less than?' Is 'twice' my age older or younger than my age now?" as he points to the left and right of 44 on the number line. (Acceptable answers are 44 x 2, 44(2), and 88.) Armando repeats the process for questions 5 and 6.

At this point in the lesson, the students are prepared to work in pairs or small groups to complete the modeled responses using their own ages. After discussing the expressions and incorporating their own ages, students practice using "n" in the mathematical expressions at the bottom of the activity sheet. Armando asks students to read through the Nora and Max questions, noticing the connections and similarities to the questions they just answered using their own ages. Armando points to discussion Sentence Starters cards on the wall and reminds students how to agree, disagree, or offer ideas when sharing their mathematical expressions with a partner. He uses this opportunity to circulate among the students, observe students' ideas, and monitor their understanding for future lesson planning.

Appendix A

This appendix contains an excerpt from WestEd's *Making Science Accessible to English Learners*, in which the 5 Es model of inquiry-based science instruction (Bybee, 1997) was discussed. The three phases of mathematics instruction presented in this guidebook (*introduce, investigate, summarize*) have much in common with the 5 Es stages of science instruction. When mathematics teachers collaborate with science teachers, this discussion of the 5 Es will be helpful in identifying areas of common instruction.

THE 5 Es MODEL OF TEACHING AND LEARNING SCIENCE

The 5 Es model represents a recursive cycle of cognitive stages in inquiry-based learning: *engage, explore, explain, elaborate,* and *evaluate*. As the arrows in Figure A.1 denote, the stages are not necessarily linear; there may well be back-and-forth progression between stages, especially between *explore* and *explain* and between *explain* and *elaborate*. The *evaluate* stage crosses into the other four as students continually reflect on what they do and do not know. Typically, not all five stages would be experienced in a single classroom period, but all five would certainly be embedded in a lesson or unit lasting days or weeks.

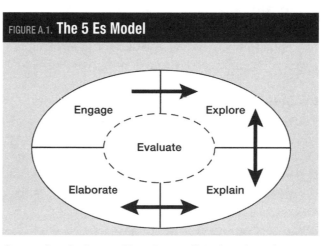

FIGURE A.1. **The 5 Es Model**

Source: Carr, J., Sexton, U., & Lagunoff, R. (2007). *Making Science Accessible to English Learners: A Guidebook for Teachers.* San Francisco, CA: WestEd.

Based on constructivist learning theory, the 5 Es approach capitalizes on hands-on activities, students' curiosity, and academic discussion among students. It should be a key part of all students' mathematics and science education, explicitly connected to target concepts and content standards and used in conjunction with other methods, including direct instruction.

Engage

The teacher starts the learning process by involving students in making connections between their past and present learning experiences. This stage is meant to create interest, generate curiosity, and raise questions and problems, helping students engage in their own learning process while facilitating opportunities for the teacher to identify students' preconceptions. At this time some misconceptions may surface, and they are acknowledged along with other brainstorming ideas. This alerts the teacher to ensure that the lesson explicitly addresses these misconceptions at the proper time, and later clearly identifies why some ideas are valid and some are not.

Explore

The teacher guides students as they investigate or perform an experiment about a phenomenon and arrive at a common understanding of certain concepts, processes, and skills. The teacher designs activities that encourage students to construct new knowledge or skills, propose preliminary predictions and hypotheses, "puzzle" through problems, and try alternatives to answer a question.

Explain

The teacher guides students as they demonstrate or explain their conceptual understanding, process skills, or behaviors. They debate alternative explanations and contrast new facts with prior misconceptions. As appropriate, the teacher directs their attention to aspects of their earlier *engage* and *explore* experiences. Students organize information into evidence-based statements, using the academic language of the discipline.

Elaborate

The teacher monitors activities and facilitates discussions that challenge and extend students' conceptual understanding and skills. Students apply what they learned to new experiences to develop, extend, connect, and deepen their understanding.

Evaluate

The teacher evaluates students' progress and students assess themselves throughout the other stages. Feedback may come from checking for understanding (e.g., with hand gestures, white boards), quizzes, student discussions, or journals, to name a few techniques. The teacher uses the feedback to reflect on the effectiveness of the lesson, making midcourse adjustments as indicated to better fit the needs and interests of students. The students use the feedback to reflect on what they understand and what they still need to learn or want to know next.

Similar to what we see in the 3-Phase Model of Mathematics Instruction, the role of the teacher in the 5 Es cycle is multifaceted. As a facilitator, the teacher nurtures creative thinking, problem solving, interaction, communication, and discovery. As a model, the teacher initiates thinking processes, inspires positive attitudes toward learning, motivates, and demonstrates skill-building techniques. Finally, as a guide, the teacher helps to bridge language gaps and foster individuality, collaboration, and personal growth. The teacher flows in and out of these various roles within each lesson, both as planned and as opportunities arise.

For a more detailed description of student and teacher roles during 5Es instruction, see Figure A.2.

FIGURE A.2. **The 5 Es Instructional Model**		
Purpose	**Teacher Role**	**Student Role**
Engage		
To initiate the lesson An engagement activity connects past and present learning experiences, anticipates new ideas, and organizes students' thinking toward standards and outcomes.	» create interest » generate curiosity » raise questions and problems » elicit responses that uncover students' current knowledge about the concept/topic	» ask questions such as "Why did this happen?" "What do I already know about this?" "What can I find out about this?" "How can this problem be solved?" » show interest in the topic
Explore		
To provide students with a common base of experiences within which current concepts, processes, and skills are identified and developed	» guide students to work together without direct instruction » observe and listen to students as they interact » ask probing questions to redirect students' investigations as needed » provide time for students to puzzle through problems » act as a consultant for students	» think creatively within the limits of the activity » test predictions and hypotheses » form new predictions and hypotheses » try alternatives to solve a problem and discuss them with others » record observations and ideas » suspend judgment » test ideas
Explain		
To focus students on a particular aspect of their prior stage experiences This stage provides opportunities for students to demonstrate their conceptual understanding and process skills. This stage may be an opportunity to introduce a concept, process, or skill.	» guide students to explain concepts and definitions in their own words » ask for justification (evidence) and clarification from students » formally provide definitions, explanations, and new vocabulary » use students' previous experiences as the basis for explaining concepts	» explain possible solutions or answers to other students » listen critically to and question respectfully other students' explanations » listen and try to comprehend explanations offered by the teacher » refer to previous activities

Purpose	Teacher Role	Student Role

Elaborate

To challenge and extend students' conceptual understanding and skills Through new experiences, students develop deeper and broader understanding, more information, and adequate skills.	» expect students to use learned academic language in a new context » encourage students to apply the concepts and skills in new situations » remind students of alternative explanations » refer students to alternative explanations	» apply new labels, definitions, explanations, and skills in new but connected situations » use previous information to ask questions, propose solutions, make decisions, and design experiments » draw reasonable conclusions from evidence » record observations or explanations

Evaluate

To encourage students to assess their understanding and abilities and to provide opportunities for teachers to evaluate student progress	» refer students to existing data and evidence and ask, "What do you already know?" "Why do you think...?" » observe students as they apply new concepts and skills » assess students' knowledge/skills » look for evidence that students have changed their thinking » ask students to assess their learning and group process skills » ask open-ended questions such as "What evidence do you have?" "What do you know about the problem?"	» check for understanding among peers » answer open-ended questions by using observations, evidence, and previously accepted explanations » demonstrate an understanding or knowledge of the concept or skill » evaluate own progress and knowledge » ask related questions that would encourage future investigations

Source: Bybee, R.W. (1997). *Achieving scientific literacy: From purposes to practices.* Portsmouth, NH: Heinemann. Adapted with permission.

Appendix B

Although the primary audience for this guidebook is middle school and high school mathematics teachers, we are aware that teachers in grades 3–5 and perhaps K–2 may find the guidebook relevant to providing English learners access to mathematics instruction. Chapter 3 contains Academic Language Skills (ALS) charts for grades 6–8 and 9–12. This appendix contains ALS charts for grades K–2 (Figure B.1) and grades 3–5 (Figure B.2).

FIGURE B.1. Academic Language Skills Grades K–2

AL Skill	Beginning	Early Intermediate	Intermediate	Early Advanced	Advanced
Listen & Respond	Listen to and follow one-step directions. Listen to teacher's simple questions, answers, and brief explanations and show understanding using nonverbal responses and a few words orally.	Listen to and follow one-step directions. Listen to teacher's simple questions, answers, and brief explanations and identify a key concept using words, phrases, or simple sentences orally.	Listen to and follow two-step directions. Listen to teacher's simple questions, answers, and brief explanations and identify an important concept and details using complete sentences.	Listen to and follow multi-step directions. Listen to teacher's simple questions, answers, and brief explanations and identify key concepts and details.	Same as Early Advanced
Use Academic Vocabulary	Use basic vocabulary to communicate needs and information in social and academic settings.	Use more vocabulary in phrases and simple sentences to communicate basic needs and information in social and academic settings.	Use more vocabulary in detailed sentences to express simple ideas in a wider variety of social and academic settings.	Use expanded academic vocabulary in detailed sentences to express ideas by asking, questioning, and restating information.	Use expanded academic vocabulary in detailed sentences to express ideas by asking, questioning, soliciting, and paraphrasing information.
Ask & Answer Questions	After teacher reads informational material aloud, show understanding and communicate questions by using nonverbal responses and a few words orally.	During assisted reading of informational material, orally ask and answer factual comprehension questions using phrases or simple sentences (subject-verb-object).	After reading informational material with some assistance, ask and answer factual comprehension questions about informational materials using simple sentences.	After reading informational material, ask and answer factual comprehension questions with some supporting details.	After reading informational material (read to in grade K), ask and answer factual comprehension questions with supporting details.
Retell Main Ideas	After teacher reads informational material, retell familiar informational materials using nonverbal responses and a few words.	During assisted reading of informational material (read to in grade K), retell using verbal phrases and some simple sentences.	After reading informational material with some assistance (read to in grade K), retell using expanded vocabulary in more detailed sentences.	After reading informational material (read to in grade K), retell with paraphrasing and some supporting details.	Retell written information with paraphrasing and supporting details.

AL Skill	Beginning	Early Intermediate	Intermediate	Early Advanced	Advanced
Write in Content Areas	Copy the English alphabet legibly; write words, perhaps with aid of word walls or other sources; illustrate ideas appropriately.	Use sentence frames to write one or two simple sentences; illustrate ideas appropriately.	Rely less on sentence frames to write simple sentences; illustrate ideas appropriately.	Use more detailed sentences; in grades 1 and 2, write connected sentences.	Write a few connected sentences in kindergarten; write short narratives in grades 1 and 2.
Use Writing Strategies	Label graphic organizers with key words to express ideas or identify vocabulary meaning.	Use labels and phrases in graphic organizers and sentence frames to express ideas as well as vocabulary meaning.	With guided use of the writing process, write sentences (grades K and 1) or short paragraphs (grade 2) to express an idea.	Use the writing process to write sentences (grades K and 1) and short paragraphs (grade 2).	Use the writing process to write clear and connected sentences (grades K and 1) and paragraphs (grade 2).
Think Critically	Use gestures and a few words to identify conclusions, compare and contrast, and identify simple sequential or chronological order (e.g., beginning, middle, end).	Use phrases to make predictions, compare and contrast, recognize cause and effect relationships, and identify sequential or chronological order.	Use sentences to make and confirm predictions, compare and contrast, recognize cause and effect relationships, and identify sequential or chronological order.	Use connected sentences with details to make and confirm predictions, compare and contrast; recognize cause and effect relationships, and identify sequential or chronological order.	Same as Early Advanced

Source: Carr, J., Sexton, U., & Lagunoff, R. (2007). *Making Science Accessible to English Learners: A Guidebook for Teachers*. San Francisco, CA: WestEd.

FIGURE B.2. Academic Language Skills Grades 3–5

AL Skill	Beginning	Early Intermediate	Intermediate	Early Advanced	Advanced
Listen & Respond	Listen to and follow simple directions. Listen to teacher's simple questions, answers, and brief explanations aided by appropriate level of scaffolds. Show understanding by identifying one or a few key ideas using gestures and phrases.	Listen to and follow more complex directions. Listen to teacher's questions, answers, and brief explanations aided by appropriate level of scaffolds. Show understanding by identifying some key ideas using simple sentences.	Listen to and follow multi-step directions. Listen to teacher's questions, answers, and explanations aided by appropriate level of scaffolds. Show understanding by describing key ideas using complete sentences with more details.	Listen to and follow multi-step directions. Listen during teacher's lesson and engage in class discussion with visual aids. Show understanding by explaining key ideas using detailed sentences.	Same as Early Advanced
Use Academic Vocabulary	Use a few academic vocabulary words in simple phrases and sentences to communicate basic meaning in social and academic settings.	Use some academic vocabulary words in sentences to communicate meaning in social and academic settings. Use context clues to understand a few unknown words.	Use expanded academic vocabulary in more detailed sentences to express ideas when asking, answering, soliciting, and restating information. Use context clues and a glossary to understand some unknown words.	Use expanded academic vocabulary in detailed sentences to express complex ideas when asking, answering, soliciting, and restating information. Use context clues and a dictionary to understand some unknown words.	Same as Early Advanced
Ask & Answer Questions	During assisted reading, orally ask and answer simple factual comprehension questions using nonverbal or simple verbal responses.	During assisted reading, orally ask and answer factual comprehension questions using phrases or simple sentences.	After reading with some assistance, ask and answer factual comprehension questions using some detailed sentences.	After reading, ask and answer factual comprehension questions using detailed sentences.	After reading grade-level materials, ask and answer factual comprehension questions using detailed sentences.

AL Skill	Beginning	Early Intermediate	Intermediate	Early Advanced	Advanced
Describe Main Ideas	During assisted reading, retell familiar informational materials and identify the main idea using nonverbal or simple verbal responses.	During assisted reading, retell familiar informational materials and identify the main idea by using phrases or simple sentences.	After reading with some assistance, describe the main idea of informational materials by using detailed sentences.	After reading, describe the main ideas of informational materials including important details.	After reading grade-appropriate informational materials, explain the main ideas by connecting to important details and using expanded vocabulary.
Write in Content Areas	Label graphic organizers using key words and phrases. Fill in sentence frames or write simple sentences.	With writing scaffolds, write an increasing number of words and simple sentences.	With writing scaffolds, write more sentences and brief narratives or compositions.	Write compositions that include a main idea and supporting details.	Write well-developed compositions that include a main idea and supporting details.
Use Writing Strategies	Create phrases or simple sentences that can be understood when read.	With guided use of the writing process, produce independent writing that is understood when read, but may include inconsistent use of standard grammatical forms.	With guided use of the writing process, create cohesive paragraphs that develop a central idea with use of many standard English grammatical forms; may include errors in grammar and conventions.	Use all of the steps of the writing process to draft clear, coherent, focused essays and reports; may include some minor errors in grammar and conventions.	Independently use all of the steps of the writing process to draft clear, coherent, focused essays and reports; may include a few minor errors in grammar and conventions.
Think Critically	Use gestures and a few words to compare and contrast, and identify simple sequential or chronological order.	Use phrases and simple sentences to make predictions, draw simple conclusions, compare and contrast, identify sequential or chronological order, and distinguish between fact and opinion.	Use more detailed sentences to make and confirm predictions, draw conclusions, make generalizations, compare and contrast, describe cause and effect relationships, describe sequential or chronological order, and distinguish between fact and opinion.	Use detailed, connected sentences to make and confirm predictions, draw conclusions, make inferences and generalizations, compare and contrast, identify cause and effect relationships, analyze sequential or chronological order, and distinguish between fact and opinion.	Same as Early Advanced

Source: Carr, J., Sexton, U., & Lagunoff, R. (2007). *Making Science Accessible to English Learners: A Guidebook for Teachers*. San Francisco, CA: WestEd.

About the Authors

JOHN W. CARR develops resource products, conducts workshops, and evaluates programs related to instruction and assessment of English learners. He developed WestEd's bestselling *Map of Standards for English Learners* for California and continues to conduct an implementation workshop for teachers and educational leaders throughout the state. He coauthored another WestEd bestseller, *Making Science Accessible to English Learners: A Guidebook for Teachers* (2007). He is also an author in the areas of standards-based grading and assessment, and using program evaluation for school improvement. He led a team that developed English language development (ELD) standards, the supporting *Idaho Map of Standards for English Learners,* and the related workshop in 2006; developed the *Idaho Guidebook for Math and Science Educators: Making Content Accessible to English Learners* and supporting workshop in 2008; and has conducted annual workshops for the Idaho State Department of Education from 2006 to 2008. He conducts evaluations of educational programs and professional development projects related to improving education for English learners. He has a BA in psychology and an MA in research psychology from California State University, Sacramento, and a PhD in educational measurement, evaluation, and research methodology from the University of California, Berkeley. John is Senior Research Associate for the Evaluation Research program at WestEd's Oakland, California, office and may be reached by email: jcarr@WestEd.org.

CATHY CARROLL is a nationally recognized leader in the mathematics education community and works with teachers and leaders throughout the country in mathematics professional development and leadership development. Cathy coauthored *Learning to Lead Mathematics Professional Development*, a video-based curriculum for developing leaders of mathematics professional development. She is currently co-Principal Investigator for a National Science Foundation-funded project, Researching Mathematics Leader Learning, and lead evaluator for WestEd's evaluation of Intel Math. Cathy served as mathematics content specialist for *Teachers as Learners: A Multimedia Kit for Professional Development in Science and Mathematics*. Previously, she was director of the Mathematics Renaissance Leadership Alliance, an initiative funded by the California Department of Education to develop teacher leadership and administrative support for quality mathematics programs. Earlier she served as associate director for Mathematics Renaissance K–12 and regional director for the Middle Grades Mathematics Renaissance. Cathy also has nearly twenty years' experience teaching middle school mathematics in the San Francisco Bay Area. She is a Senior Project Director in the Mathematics, Science & Technology program at WestEd's Redwood City, California, office and may be reached by email: ccarroll@WestEd.org.

SARAH CREMER contributes to the development, implementation, and research of mathematics and science curricula. She is currently developing curriculum for the *Algebraic Interventions for Measured Achievement* (AIMA) program. AIMA is an algebra intervention curriculum funded by the U.S. Department of Education's Institute of Education Sciences (IES) that targets specific algebraic learning trouble spots. She also participates in projects related to teacher education and preparation, and assessment development and application. She has presented nationally on mathematics learning and teaching. She has taught mathematics to elementary, middle, and high school students at all levels of achievement and in school and after-school settings. Her primary areas of interest include student and teacher learning within the classroom. She received a BS in mathematics from Bates College and an MA in mathematics education from the University of California, Berkeley. Sarah is a Research Assistant for the Mathematics, Science, & Technology program at WestEd. She may be reached at WestEd's Redwood City, California, office or by email: scremer@WestEd.org.

MARDI A. GALE is a curriculum developer, and designs and facilitates professional development at WestEd. She is the principal author of the *Aim for Algebra* intervention curriculum and the director of the professional development supporting the program. She contributed to the *Idaho Guidebook for Math and Science Educators: Making Content Accessible to English Learners*, in collaboration with John Carr. After more than 20 years of teaching and facilitating professional development, Mardi was invited to be a regional director for the Middle Grades Mathematics Renaissance, a component of California's State Systemic Initiative. She served as a regional director for the Mathematics Renaissance K–12 program, then as an associate director for the Mathematics Renaissance Leadership Alliance. As an instructor for math content courses for teachers at the University of California, Los Angeles, Mardi worked with teachers at all levels to enhance their mathematical content knowledge. She has participated in many facets of cutting edge assessment, as a member of the Mathematics Development Team for the California Assessment Program and the New Standards Project. Mardi was also honored as presenter at the National Summit for Assessment. At WestEd, she was an evaluator of the California Mathematics Professional Development Institutes and participates as a consultant at academic audits for the Comprehensive School Assistance Program. Email: mgale@WestEd.org

RACHEL LAGUNOFF develops, reviews, and aligns standards and assessments, with a focus on improving the academic outcomes of English learners. She has provided expertise in research studies and services for several states, as well as national groups. She was a reviewer for the *Framework for High-Quality English Language Proficiency Standards and Assessments* and is coauthor of the bestselling *Map of Standards for English Learners* and *Making Science Accessible to English Learners: A Guidebook for Teachers.* She was codeveloper of English language development (ELD) standards and supporting *Idaho Map of Standards for English Learners,* as well as the *Idaho Guidebook for Math and Science Educators: Making Content Accessible to English Learners.* She has taught university courses in linguistics, applied linguistics, and English as a second language. She received an MA in teaching English as a second language and a PhD in applied linguistics, both from the University of California, Los Angeles. Rachel is Senior Research Associate for the Assessment and Standards Development Services program at WestEd. She may be reached at WestEd's San Francisco office or by email: rlaguno@WestEd.org.

URSULA M. SEXTON conducts research and manages projects that investigate the roles that cultural diversity and language play in mathematics and science assessment development, testing, and instructional practices. She also contributes to projects involving teacher accreditation, school reform, systemic professional development, science and mathematics curriculum, access of academic content for English learners, and the use of technology in education. She is coauthor of *Making Science Accessible to English Learners: A Guidebook for Teachers* and co-developer of the professional development to support the *Idaho Guidebook for Math and Science Educators: Making Content Accessible to English Learners.* She has served on federal and state science education panels and as a reviewer of National Science Foundation programs. As a former bilingual/science teacher and teacher educator, she represented the profession as the 1994 California Presidential Awardee for Excellence in Mathematics and Science Teaching, the 1998 National Science Teacher of the Year, and the 1999 California State University-Hayward Teacher of the Year. She holds a BA in biological sciences from Holy Names College, and a multiple-subject teaching credential with bilingual emphasis (Spanish) and a life science K–8 certification from California State University, Hayward. Ursula is Senior Research Associate for the Culture and Language in Education project and the Mathematics, Science, and Technology program at WestEd. She may be reached at WestEd's Redwood City, California office or by email: usexton@WestEd.org.

Also Available from WestEd

Aim for Algebra™ Intervention Curriculum & Professional Development

Who Should Adopt *Aim for Algebra* Curriculum?

» Teachers of algebra, algebra intervention, and algebra readiness courses
» After-school, extended day, and summer school algebra teachers
» High school exit exam preparation classes
» District/site personnel responsible for mathematics curriculum and programs

What Is *Aim for Algebra* All About?

Aim for Algebra is a standards-aligned, concept-based supplemental/intervention curriculum developed by WestEd with funding from the U.S. Department of Education's Institute of Education Sciences. The curriculum is a coherent set of conceptual materials rather than a collection of worksheets on individual topics.

In *Aim for Algebra*, WestEd researchers address common barriers to learning algebra. This targeted curriculum helps students understand essential math topics through learning experiences that reinforce, refresh, or reteach these important concepts.

Aim for Algebra has a modular format for easy implementation, flexible programming, and individualized student placement. The content-specific modules may be accessed as a complete set, individually, or as replacement materials, allowing teachers to provide students a variety of experiences in regular, intervention, or readiness algebra classes.

Aim for Algebra lessons are based on cognitive research and learning theory to optimize students' understanding and retention and enable them to bridge the conceptual gaps found in traditional algebra curricula. Lessons feature:

» A focus on the typical barriers to success in algebra
» Purposeful sequencing and scaffolding of ideas to promote deeper comprehension
» Multiple strategies to reduce student misconceptions
» Manipulatives for hands-on learning for students with varying learning styles

Each module includes a student workbook, lesson-by-lesson facilitator guide, pre/post tests, answer keys, and appropriate manipulatives.

On-site implementation seminars with flexible dates are available for school or district teams. The on-site institutes take place over three days: an initial two-day implementation seminar and a one-day follow-up later in the year. Multiple-day seminars, on-site coaching, and technical assistance services are also available.

For more information, contact Kimberly Viviani at 650.381.6429 or kviviani@WestEd.org; or visit us online at www.WestEd.org/aimforalgebra.

Also Available from WestEd

Math Pathways & Pitfalls Intervention Curriculum

Who Should Use the *Math Pathways & Pitfalls* Curriculum?

» K–7 classroom teachers
» After-school, extended day, and summer school teachers
» Teachers with English learners in their classrooms
» District/site personnel responsible for mathematics curriculum and programs

What is *Math Pathways & Pitfalls*?

Math Pathways & Pitfalls (*MPP*) is a research-based intervention curriculum that fosters students' ability to represent and reason about mathematical concepts, and explicitly calls their attention to common misconceptions or pitfalls. *MPP* materials are designed to jump-start discussion-based instruction with diverse learners, including English learners. At each grade level, *MPP* addresses 10 to 12 of the toughest mathematics concepts, such as place value, subtraction, fractions, and percentages. Developed with funding from the Stuart Foundation and the National Science Foundation, *Math Pathways & Pitfalls* has been shown to boost student achievement for both native English speakers and English language learners.

What Is Included in the Curriculum?

Each *Math Pathways & Pitfalls* book contains lessons for two grade levels, including engaging teaching guides and black line masters for student pages; a DVD containing a video for students and video for teachers; a CD with black line masters and resources for all student materials; a classroom *Discussion Builders* poster; and teacher professional development tasks to do individually or with colleagues.

> *Math Pathways & Pitfalls* Lessons and Teaching Manual
> Number Sense and Operations with Algebra Readiness
> Units K and 1 • ISBN: 978-0-914409-58-8

> *Math Pathways & Pitfalls* Lessons and Teaching Manual
> Number Sense and Operations with Algebra Readiness
> Units 2 and 3 • ISBN: 978-0-914409-59-5

> *Math Pathways & Pitfalls* Lessons and Teaching Manual
> Fractions and Decimals with Algebra Readiness
> Units 4 and 5 • ISBN: 978-0-914409-60-1

> *Math Pathways & Pitfalls* Lessons and Teaching Manual
> Percents, Ratios, and Proportions with Algebra Readiness
> Units 6 and 7 • ISBN: 978-0-914409-61-8

Professional development and technical assistance are available. For more information about Math Pathways & Pitfalls, visit WestEd.org/mpp. To order materials, please email WestEd: info@WestEd.org.

Also Available from WestEd

Math Pathways & Pitfalls Institutes

What are *Math Pathways and Pitfalls* Institutes?

Math Pathways and Pitfalls Institutes help K–7 teachers use *Math Pathways and Pitfalls* (*MPP*) strategies and materials along with their district-adopted curriculum. Studies show that *MPP* lessons and strategies can have a positive impact on learning in diverse classrooms.

MPP Institutes show teachers strategies to help students:

» Turn common mathematics pitfalls into pathways for learning
» Develop mathematical language
» Be part of a community of learners
» Learn mathematical content through multiple modalities

Who Should Attend *Math Pathways and Pitfalls* Institutes?

Anyone who is using or considering using *Math Pathways & Pitfalls* intervention curriculum including:

» K–8 classroom, after-school, and summer school teachers who want practical, evidence-based strategies and tools that help students learn standards-based mathematics content and develop academic language skills
» Teachers who have diverse learners, including English learners, in their classrooms
» Professional developers and instructional coaches

National Science Foundation Experimental Study

Findings from a large-scale randomized trial demonstrated that teaching only seven *Math Pathways & Pitfalls* lessons, in conjunction with the regular mathematics curriculum, boosts the achievement of both native English speakers and English learners.

For information on cost, pricing, and materials, please contact Alma Ramirez at 510.302.4249 or aramire@WestEd.org.

Also Available from WestEd

Discussion Builders Posters and Teaching Guides
K–1, 2–3, and 4–8

By talking to learn, students also learn how to think. The sentence stems on these colorful posters provide students with a scaffold for voicing their ideas and questions, valuing others' contributions, and using increasingly sophisticated thinking strategies. *Discussion Builders* help students learn through active participation in classroom discussions. Accompanying quick-guides for teachers explain how to get students talking — and thinking — more conceptually, in any subject.

Proven powerful for English language learners and students of all achievement levels, *Discussion Builders* scaffold progressively more complex reasoning. In grades K–1, the focus is on helping students present, expand, and reflect on important ideas. In grades 2–3, *Discussion Builders* prompt students to use these skills at more sophisticated levels. The grades 4–8 poster helps strengthen complex reasoning, including their abilities to consider counterexamples and conjectures and to justify options.

Carne Clarke and Alma Ramirez

Discussion Builders Poster & Teaching Guide: K-1 • $14.95 • 24 x 36 • 2005 • MATH-05-01
Discussion Builders Poster & Teaching Guide: 2-3 • $14.95 • 24 x 36 • 2005 • MATH-05-02
Discussion Builders Poster & Teaching Guide: 4-8 • $14.95 • 24 x 36 • 2005 • MATH-05-03
Set • $38.00 • 2005 • MATH-05-04 (Save 15% off the individual price by ordering the set.)

Also Available from WestEd

Discussion Builders Workshop

Who Should Attend

K–8 classroom teachers who want practical, evidence-based teaching strategies that foster oral and written academic language development. Excellent for teachers with English learners in their classroom.

What Are Discussion Builders?

Originally created for teaching math, *Discussion Builders* is a suite of classroom posters, teaching guides, and classroom strategies, developed and field-tested with funding from the National Science Foundation. *Discussion Builders* promotes academic language by helping students build reasoning and communications skills. Sentence stems on the posters provide students with a scaffold for voicing their ideas and questions and valuing others' contributions. The teaching guide includes tasks and blackline masters for using the *Discussion Builders* in any subject area.

What Teachers Learn

» Powerful, easy-to-implement strategies using National Science Foundation-funded, field-tested *Discussion Builders* classroom posters and teaching guide

» Proven techniques for building students' communication and reasoning skills

» Practical ways to help all students overcome academic, linguistic, and social barriers in classroom discussions

» Overview of current research on the role of academic language development in academic success

» Practice facilitating productive discussions in mathematics, literature, social studies, and other content areas

For more information, contact Kate D. Darling at 510.302.4253 or kdarlin@WestEd.org; or visit us online at www.WestEd.org/discussionbuilders.

Also Available
from WestEd

Making Science Accessible to English Learners
A Guidebook for Teachers, Updated Edition

This updated edition of the best-selling guidebook helps middle and high school science teachers reach English learners in their classrooms. The guide offers practical guidance, powerful and concrete strategies, and sample lesson scenarios that can be implemented immediately in any science class. It includes:

» Rubrics to help teachers identify the most important language skills at five ELD levels
» Practical guidance and tips from the field
» Seven scaffolding strategies for differentiating instruction
» Seven tools to promote academic language and scientific discourse
» Assessment techniques and accommodations to lower communication barriers for English learners
» Two integrated lesson scenarios demonstrating how to combine and embed these various strategies, tools, techniques, and approaches

The volume is designed for teachers who have had limited preparation for teaching science in classrooms where some students are also English learners.

Chapter topics include understanding language development, teaching the language of scientists, scaffolding science learning, and applying strategies in the classroom.

John Carr, Ursula Sexton, and Rachel Lagunoff
$24.95 • 132 pages • Trade paper • 8.5 x 11 • 2007 • WestEd •
978-0-914409-40-3 • CC-07-01

www.WestEd.org/makingscienceaccessible

To read "Chapter 6: Assessing English Learners," visit
www.WestEd.org/makingscienceaccessible.

Also Available from WestEd

The Making Science Accessible to English Learners
Workshop and Professional Development

Who Should Attend

» Science teachers grades 6–12 (may include grades 4–5)
» Secondary level English language development (ELD) and science leaders, coaches, staff developers

Goals of the Workshop

Science teachers enhance their knowledge and skills to differentiate instruction and assessment for diverse learners, particularly English learners, thereby giving all students universal, equitable access to a rigorous science curriculum. School and district leaders blend the workshop into an ongoing professional support system for teachers.

Workshop Formats

Full-day workshop participants engage in a hands-on lesson as the facilitator models effective teaching practices based on WestEd's *Making Science Accessible to English Learners: A Guidebook for Teachers, Updated Edition.* Participants have many opportunities for questioning, inquiring, reflecting, and problem solving with each other and the facilitator.

Half-day workshops focus on instructional strategies and offer streamlined hands-on learning.

Please inquire about customized workshops that delve deeper into differentiated instructional strategies and classroom management, and classroom assessment that allows English learners to demonstrate what they have learned.

What You Learn

» How to tailor the five Es (Engage, Explore, Explain, Elaborate, Evaluate) into an inquiry-based approach to teaching science to English learners
» How to use a chart of eight essential language skills to plan lessons that include English learners at different English language development levels
» An approach for teaching and applying academic language during lessons
» Seven research-based strategies as scaffolds to help students meet rigorous content standards
» Accommodations for equitable assessments
» How to integrate the instructional tools and strategies into "doable" daily pedagogy

For more information, contact John Carr at jcarr@WestEd.org or Ursula Sexton at usexton@WestEd.org.

Also Available from WestEd

Making Mathematics Accessible to English Learners
Workshops and Professional Development

Who Should Participate?

» Upper elementary, middle, and high school mathematics teachers
» Mathematics coaches
» Staff developers
» Mathematics instructional leaders.

What Do Participants Learn?

Using the principles and approaches described in *Making Mathematics Accessible to English Learners: A Guidebook for Teachers,* WestEd offers workshops and professional development for schools and districts. Sessions include topics such as:

» How to tailor the Three-Phase Model of mathematics instruction to support an inquiry-based approach to teaching mathematics to English learners
» How to use a chart of eight essential language skills to plan lessons that include English learners at different English language development levels
» An approach for teaching and applying academic language during mathematics lessons
» Seven research-based strategies to scaffold rigorous mathematics content standards
» Accommodations to design equitable classroom mathematics assessments
» How to integrate the instructional tools and strategies into "doable" daily instruction

Participants enhance their knowledge and skills to differentiate instruction and assessment for diverse learners, particularly English learners, thereby giving all students universal, equitable access to a rigorous mathematics curriculum. School and district leaders blend the workshop into an ongoing professional support system for teachers.

For information about the workshops, customized training, or technical assistance, contact WestEd:

Cathy Carroll
Tel: 650.381.6422
ccarrol@WestEd.org

John Carr
Tel: 925.673.0801
jcarr@WestEd.org